Meeting the Needs

of Your Most Able Pupils:

GEOGRAPHY

Other titles in the series

Meeting the Needs of Your Most Able Pupils: Art
Kim Earle
1 84312 331 2
978 1 84312 331 6

Meeting the Needs of Your Most Able Pupils: Design and Technology
Louise T. Davies
1 84312 330 4
978 1 84312 330 9

Meeting the Needs of Your Most Able Pupils: History
Steven Barnes
1 84312 287 1
978 1 84312 287 6

Meeting the Needs of Your Most Able Pupils: Mathematics
Lynne McClure and Jennifer Piggott
1 84312 328 2
978 1 84312 328 6

Meeting the Needs of Your Most Able Pupils: Music
Jonathan Savage
1 84312 347 9
978 1 84312 347 7

Meeting the Needs of Your Most Able Pupils: Physical Education and Sport
David Morley and Richard Bailey
1 84312 334 7
978 1 84312 334 7

Meeting the Needs

of Your Most Able Pupils:

GEOGRAPHY

Jane Ferretti

Routledge
Taylor & Francis Group

LONDON AND NEW YORK

First published 2007 by
Routledge
2 Park Square, Milton Park, Abingdon, Oxon OX14 4RN

Simultaneously published in the USA and Canada by
Routledge
270 Madison Ave, New York, NY 10016

Routledge is an imprint of Taylor & Francis, an informa business

British Library Cataloguing in Publication data
A catalogue record for this book is available from the British Library

Library of Congress Cataloging in Publication Data
A catalog record has been requested

ISBN 13: 978 1 84312 335 4 (pbk)
ISBN 13: 978 0 2 3 93526 2 (ebk)
ISBN 10: 1 84312 335 5 (pbk)
ISBN 10: 0 203 93526 8 (ebk)

Series production editors: Sarah Fish and Andrew Welsh
Typeset by Servis Filmsetting Ltd, Manchester
Printed and bound in Great Britain
by Bell & Bain Ltd, Glasgow

Contents

Acknowledgements

Meeting the Needs of Your Most Able Pupils: Geography is one outcome of the Geographical Association's Valuing Places project, funded by the Department for International Development (DfID) and the Tubney Foundation. The authors are grateful for the support of this project and particularly to Diane Swift, who coordinated the Valuing Places project and provided support in the form of comments and advice as the manuscript for this book developed. Diane was project leader for continuing professional development at the Geographical Association (GA).

Particular thanks go to Jeremy Reynolds and Chris Stevens who contributed extensively to this book. Jeremy wrote Chapter 3 and Chris wrote Chapter 2, and both were involved in discussions and made extensive contributions to all aspects of the project.

Jeremy Reynolds is Hertfordshire county adviser for gifted and talented, working with primary, secondary and special schools to improve the provision for these students both inside and beyond the classroom. Before taking up this post he was assistant head teacher at Stanborough School, Welwyn Garden City, and head of geography and head of sixth form at Simon Balle School in Hertford. He has been involved in running gifted and talented summer schools and masterclasses and also organised an extensive fieldwork programme for pupils in Britain and abroad. In March 2000, he delivered a lecture at the Royal Geographical Society (RGS) on running a successful geography department.

Chris Stevens has taught at the Minster School, Southwell, Nottinghamshire, for 12 years and is currently assistant head teacher: director of school specialism. The school has specialist status for music and humanities, and geography is the lead subject. Chris has also worked closely with PGCE students from the University of Nottingham and has contributed to a number of geography textbooks. He assisted in the production of training materials for Key Stage 3 National Strategy Toolkits including video footage.

Thanks to Rob Lodge, who works as a secondary strategy foundation subjects adviser for Norfolk Education Advisory Services and who also made valuable contributions to the project.

Contributors to the series

The author

Jane Ferretti is a lecturer in education at the University of Sheffield working in initial teacher training. Until 2003 she was head of geography at King Edward VII School, Sheffield, a large 11–18 comprehensive, and was also involved in gifted and talented initiatives at the school and with the local authority. Jane has co-authored a number of A level geography textbooks and a GCSE revision book and is one of the editors of *Wideworld* magazine. She is a member of the Geographical Association and a contributor to their journals *Teaching Geography* and *Geography*.

Series editor

Gwen Goodhew's many and varied roles within the field of gifted and talented education have included school G&T coordinator, director of Wirral Able Children Centre, Knowsley Excellence in Cities (EiC) G&T coordinator, member of the DfES G&T Advisory Group, teacher trainer and consultant. She has written and edited numerous reports and articles on the subject and co-authored *Providing for Able Children* with Linda Evans.

Other authors

Art

Kim Earle is a former secondary head of art and design and is currently an able pupils and arts consultant for St Helens. She has been a member of DfES steering groups, is an Artsmark validator, a subject editor for G&TWISE and a practising designer jeweller and enameller.

Design and Technology

During the writing of the book **Louise T. Davies** was a part-time subject adviser for design and technology at the QCA (Qualifications and Curriculum Authority), and part of the KS3 National Strategy team for the D&T programme. She has authored over 40 D&T books and award-winning multimedia resources. She is currently deputy chief executive of the Design and Technology Association.

History

Steven Barnes is a former head of history at a secondary school and Secondary Strategy consultant for the School Improvement Service in Lincolnshire. He has written history exemplifications for Assessment for Learning for the Secondary National Strategy. He is now an assistant head with responsibility for teaching and learning for a school in Lincolnshire.

Mathematics

Lynne McClure is an independent consultant in the field of mathematics education and G&T. She works with teachers and students in schools all over the UK and abroad as well as Warwick, Cambridge, Oxford Brookes and Edinburgh Universities. Lynne edits several maths and education journals.

Jennifer Piggott is a lecturer in mathematics enrichment and communication technology at Cambridge University. She is Director of the NRICH mathematics project and is part of the eastern region coordination team for the NCETM (National Centre for Excellence in the Teaching of Mathematics). Jennifer is an experienced mathematics and ICT teacher.

Music

Jonathan Savage is a senior lecturer in music education at the Institute of Education, Manchester Metropolitan University. Until 2001 he was head of music at Debenham High School, an 11–16 comprehensive school in Suffolk. He is a co-author of a new resource introducing computer game sound design to the Key Stage 3 curriculum (www.sound2game.net) and managing director of UCan.tv (www.ucan.tv), a company specialising in the production of educational software and hardware. When not doing all of this, he is busy parenting four very musically talented children!

Physical Education and Sport

David Morley has taught physical education in a number of secondary schools. He is currently senior lecturer in physical education at Leeds Metropolitan University and the director of the national DfES-funded 'Development in PE' project which is part of the Gifted and Talented strand of the PE, School Sport and Club Links (PESSCL) project. He is also a member of the team responsible for developing resources for national Multi-skill Clubs and is the founder and director of the Carnegie Regional Multi-skill Camp held at Leeds Met Carnegie.

Richard Bailey is professor of pedagogy at Roehampton University, having previously worked at Reading and Leeds Metropolitan University, and at Canterbury Christ Church University where he was director of the Centre for Physical Education Research. He is a well-known author and speaker on physical education, sport and education.

Online content on the Routledge website

The material accompanying this book may be used by the purchasing individual/organisation only. The files may be amended to suit particular situations, or individual learning needs, and printed out for use by the purchaser. The material can be accessed at www.routledge.com/education/fultonresources.asp.

01 Institutional quality standards in gifted and talented education
02 Geography provision – a checklist for consideration
03 An audit of provision for more able students in geography
04 Audit of learning styles with focus on provision for more able students
05 Geography department action plan for improving provision for more able students (annual)
06 Lesson observation schedule: gifted and talented focus
07 Monitoring and evaluation: student work analysis feedback
08 Monitoring and evaluation: scheme of work feedback
09 Geography progress report
10 Monitoring and evaluation: departmental review and report
11 Geography department: individual pupil checklist
12 Rapid checklist for identifying more able pupils in geography
13 VAK Questionnaire for use with pupils
14 'Pole to Pole': an open-ended task incorporating choice and encouraging research
15 Scheme of work – Key Stage 3: Development and globalisation
16 Extended writing task based on card-sorting exercise
17 Webquest: Nike (clothing) – are they just doing it?
18 Census data – Sheffield
19 Programme for summer school

www.routledge.com/education

Introduction

Who should use this book?

This book is for all teachers of geography working with Key Stage 3 and Key Stage 4 pupils. It will be relevant to teachers working within the full spectrum of schools, from highly selective establishments to comprehensive and secondary modern schools as well as some special schools. Its overall objective is to provide a practical resource that heads of department, gifted and talented coordinators, leading teachers for gifted and talented education and classroom teachers can use to develop a coherent approach to provision for their most able pupils.

Why is it needed?

School populations differ greatly and pupils considered very able in one setting might not stand out in another. Nevertheless, whatever the general level of ability within a school, there has been a tendency to plan and provide for the middle range, to modify for those who are struggling and to leave the most able to 'get on with it'. This has meant that the most able have:

- not been sufficiently challenged and stimulated

- underachieved

- been unaware of what they might be capable of achieving

- been unaware of what they need to do to achieve at the highest level

- not had high enough ambitions and aspirations

- sometimes become disaffected.

How will this book help teachers?

This book and its accompanying website will, through its combination of practical ideas, materials for photocopying or downloading, and case studies:

- help teachers of geography to focus on the top 5–10% of the ability range in their particular school and to find ways of providing for these pupils, both within and beyond the classroom

- equip them with strategies and ideas to support exceptionally able pupils, i.e. those in the top 5% nationally.

Terminology

Since there is confusion about the meaning of the words 'gifted' and 'talented', the terms 'more able', 'most able' and 'exceptionally able' will generally be used in this series.

When 'gifted' and 'talented' are used, the definitions provided by the Department for Education and Skills (DfES) in its Excellence in Cities programme will apply. That is:

- **gifted** pupils are the most academically able in a school. This ability might be general or specific to a particular subject area, such as mathematics.

- **talented** pupils are those with high ability or potential in art, music, performing arts or sport.

The two groups together should form 5–10% of any school population.

There are, of course, some pupils who are both gifted and talented. Examples that come to mind are the budding physicist who plays the violin to a high standard in his spare time, or the pupil with high general academic ability who plays for the area football team.

This book is part of a series dealing with providing challenge for the most able secondary age pupils in a range of subjects. It is likely that some of the books in the series might also contain ideas that would be relevant to teachers of geography.

CHAPTER 1

Our more able pupils – the national scene

- Making good provision for the most able – what's in it for schools?
- National initiatives since 1997
- *Every Child Matters* and the Children Act 2004
- *Higher Standards, Better Schools for All* – Education White Paper, October 2005
- Self-evaluation and inspection
- Resources for teachers and parents of more able pupils

Today's gifted pupils are tomorrow's social, intellectual, economic and cultural leaders and their development cannot be left to chance.

(Deborah Eyre, director of the National Academy for Gifted and Talented Youth, 2004)

The debate about whether to make special provision for the most able pupils in secondary schools ran its course during the last decade of the twentieth century. Explicit provision to meet their learning needs is now considered neither elitist nor a luxury. From an inclusion angle these pupils must have the same chances as others to develop their potential to the full. We know from international research that focusing on the needs of the most able changes teachers' perceptions of the needs of all their pupils, and there follows a consequential rise in standards. But for teachers who are not convinced by the inclusion or school improvement arguments, there is a much more pragmatic reason for meeting the needs of able pupils. Of course, it is preferable that colleagues share a common willingness to address the needs of the most able, but if they don't, it can at least be pointed out that, quite simply, it is something that all teachers are now required to do, not an optional extra.

All schools should seek to create an atmosphere in which to excel is not only acceptable but desirable.

(*Excellence in Schools* – DfEE 1997)

> High achievement is determined by 'the school's commitment to inclusion and the steps it takes to ensure that every pupil does as well as possible'.
>
> (*Handbook for Inspecting Secondary Schools* – Ofsted 2003)

A few years ago, efforts to raise standards in schools concentrated on getting as many pupils as possible over the Level 5 hurdle at the end of Key Stage 3 and over the 5 A*–C grades hurdle at GCSE. Resources were pumped into borderline pupils and the most able were not, on the whole, considered a cause for concern. The situation has changed dramatically in the last nine years with schools being expected to set targets for A*s and As and to show added value by helping pupils entering the school with high SATs scores to achieve Levels 7 and beyond, if supporting data suggests that that is what is achievable. Early recognition of high potential and the setting of curricular targets are at last addressing the lack of progress demonstrated by many able pupils in Year 7 and more attention is being paid to creating a climate in which learning can flourish. But there is a push for even more support for the most able through the promotion of personalised learning.

> The goal is that five years from now: gifted and talented students progress in line with their ability rather than their age; schools inform parents about tailored provision in an annual school profile; curricula include a gifted and talented dimension and at 14–19 there is more stretch and differentiation at the top end, so no matter what your talent it will be engaged; and the effect of poverty on achievement is reduced, because support for high-ability students from poorer backgrounds enables them to thrive.
>
> (Speech at National Academy for Gifted and Talented Youth – David Miliband, Minister for State for School Standards, May 2004)

It is hoped that this book, with the others in this series, will help to accelerate these changes.

Making good provision for the most able – what's in it for schools?

Schools and/or subject departments often approach provision for the most able pupils with some reluctance because they imagine a lot of extra work for very little reward. In fact, the rewards of providing for these pupils are substantial.

- It can be very stimulating to the subject specialist to explore ways of developing approaches with enthusiastic and able students.

  > Taking a serious look at what I should expect from the most able and then at how I should teach them has given my teaching a new lease of life. I feel so sorry for youngsters who were taught by me ten years ago. They must have been bored beyond belief. But then, to be quite honest, so was I.
  >
  > (Science teacher)

- Offering opportunities to tackle work in a more challenging manner often interests pupils whose abilities have gone unnoticed because they have not been motivated by a bland educational diet.

  > Some of the others were invited to an after-school maths club. When I heard what they were doing, it sounded so interesting that I asked the maths teacher if I could go too. She was a bit doubtful at first because I have messed about a lot but she agreed to take me on trial. I'm one of her star pupils now and she reckons I'll easily get an A*. I still find some of the lessons really slow and boring but I don't mess around – well, not too much.
  >
  > (Year 10 boy)

- When pupils are engaged by the work they are doing motivation, attainment and discipline improve.

  > You don't need to be gifted to work out that the work we do is much more interesting and exciting. It's made others want to be like us.
  >
  > (Comment of a student involved in an extension programme for the most able)

- Schools identified as very good by Ofsted generally have good provision for their most able students.

  > If you are willing to deal effectively with the needs of able pupils you will raise the achievement of all pupils.
  >
  > (Mike Tomlinson, former director of Ofsted)

- The same is true of individual departments in secondary schools. All those considered to be very good have spent time developing a sound working approach that meets the needs of their most able pupils.

  > The department creates a positive atmosphere by its organisation, display and the way that students are valued. Learning is generally very good and often excellent throughout the school. The teachers' high expectations permeate the atmosphere and are a significant factor in raising achievement. These expectations are reflected in the curriculum which has depth and students are able and expected to experience difficult problems in all year groups.
  >
  > (Mathematics Department, Hamstead Hall School, Birmingham; Ofsted 2003)

National initiatives since 1997

In 1997, the new government demonstrated its commitment to gifted and talented education by setting up a Gifted and Talented Advisory Group (GTAG). Since then there has been a wide range of government and government-funded initiatives that have, either directly or indirectly, impacted on our most able pupils and their teachers. Details of some can be found below. Others that relate to geography will be found later in this book.

Excellence in Cities

In an attempt to deal with the chronic underachievement of able pupils in inner city areas, Excellence in Cities (EiC) was launched in 1999. This was a very ambitious, well-funded programme with many different strands. In the first place it concentrated on secondary age pupils but work was extended into the primary sector in many areas. Provision for gifted and talented students was one of the strands.

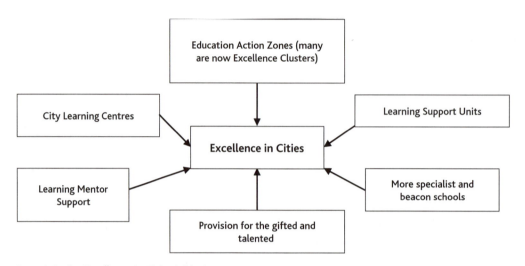

Strands in the Excellence in Cities Initiative

EiC schools were expected to:

- develop a whole-school policy for their most able pupils

- appoint a gifted and talented coordinator with sufficient time to fulfil the role

- send the coordinator on a national training programme run by Oxford Brookes University

- identify 5–10% of pupils in each year group as their gifted and talented cohort, the gifted being the academically able and the talented being those with latent or obvious ability in PE, sport, music, art or the performing arts

- provide an appropriate programme of work both within the school day and beyond

- set 'aspirational' targets both for the gifted and talented cohort as a whole and for individual pupils

- work with other schools in a 'cluster' to provide further support for these pupils

- work with other agencies, such as Aimhigher, universities, businesses and private sector schools, to enhance provision and opportunities for these pupils.

Funding changes have meant that schools no longer receive dedicated EiC money through local authorities but the lessons learned from EiC have been influential in developing a national approach to gifted and talented education. **All** schools are now expected to adopt similar strategies to ensure that the needs of their most able students are met.

Excellence Clusters

Although EiC was set up initially in the main urban conurbations, other hot spots of underachievement and poverty were also identified and Excellence Clusters were established. For example, Ellesmere Port, Crewe and Barrow-in-Furness are pockets of deprivation, with major social problems and significant underachievement, in otherwise affluent areas. Excellence Clusters have been established in these three places and measures are being taken to improve provision for the most able pupils. The approach is similar to that used in Excellence in Cities areas.

Aimhigher

Aimhigher is another initiative of the Department for Education and Skills (DfES) working in partnership with the Higher Education Funding Council for England (HEFCE). Its remit is to widen participation in UK higher education, particularly among students from groups that do not have a tradition of going to university, such as some ethnic minorities, the disabled and those from poorer homes. Both higher education institutions and secondary schools have Aimhigher coordinators who work together to identify pupils who would benefit from additional support and to plan a programme of activities. Opportunities are likely to include:

- mentoring, including e-mentoring
- residential summer schools
- visits to different campuses and university departments
- masterclasses
- online information for students and parents
- advice on the wide range of financial and other support available to disadvantaged students.

One national Aimhigher project, Higher Education Gateway, is specifically targeted on gifted and talented students from disadvantaged groups. More information can be found at www.aimhigher.ac.uk.

National Academy for Gifted and Talented Youth (NAGTY)

Government initiatives have not been confined to the most able pupils in deprived areas. In 2002, the National Academy for Gifted and Talented Youth was established at Warwick University. Its brief was to offer support to the most able 5% of the school population and their teachers and parents. It did this in a number of ways:

National Academy for Gifted and Talented Youth		
Student Academy	**Professional Academy**	**Expertise Centre**
• Summer schools including link-ups with CTY in USA. • Outreach courses in a wide range of subjects at universities and other venues across the country. • Online activities – currently maths, classics, ethics, philosophy.	• Continuing professional development for teachers. • A PGCE+ programme for trainee teachers. • Ambassador School Programme to disseminate good practice amongst schools.	• Leading research in gifted and talented education.

NAGTY worked closely with the DfES with the latter setting policy and NAGTY increasingly taking the lead in the practical application of this policy – a policy known as the English Model, which, as explained on NAGTY's website, is 'rooted in day-to-day classroom provision and enhanced by additional, more advanced opportunities offered both within school and outside of it'. NAGTY ceased operation in August 2007 and was replaced by the Young, Gifted & Talented Programme (see below).

The Young, Gifted & Talented Programme (YG&T)

In December 2006, the UK government announced the creation of a new programme in England, the National Programme for Gifted and Talented Education (NPGATE), to be managed by CfBT Education Trust and now known as the Young, Gifted & Talented Programme (YG&T). Among the changes proposed are:

- a much greater emphasis on school and local level provision.

- the setting-up of Excellence Hubs – HEI-led partnerships to provide non-residential summer schools and a diverse range of outreach provision, including summer activities, weekend events and online and blended learning models. There will be free places for the disadvantaged.

- the appointment of gifted and talented leading teachers – one for each secondary school and each cluster of primary schools.

- a national training programme for gifted and talented leading teachers organised by the national primary and secondary strategies.

Further information about YG&T can be found at www.dfes.gov.uk/ygt or www.cfbt.com.

Gifted and talented summer schools

Education authorities are encouraged to work in partnership with schools to run a number of summer schools (dependent on the size of the authority) for the most able pupils in Years 6–11. It is expected that there will be a particular emphasis on transition and that around 50 hours of tuition will be offered. Some schools and authorities run summer schools for up to ten days whilst others cover a shorter period and have follow-up sessions or even residential weekends later in the school year. Obviously the main aim is to challenge and stimulate these pupils but the DfES also hopes that:

- they will encourage teachers and advisers to adopt innovative teaching approaches

- teachers will continue to monitor these pupils over time

- where Year 6 pupils are involved, it will make secondary teachers aware of what they can achieve and raise their expectations of Year 7 pupils.

More can be found out about these summer schools at www.standards.dfes.gov. uk/giftedandtalented. Funding for them has now been incorporated into the school development grant.

Regional partnerships

When Excellence in Cities (EiC) was first introduced, gifted and talented strand coordinators from different EiC partnerships began to meet up with others in their regions to explore ways of working together so that the task would be more manageable and resources could be pooled. One of the most successful examples of cooperation was the Trans-Pennine Group that started up in the northwest. It began to organise training on a regional basis as well as masterclasses and other activities for some gifted and talented pupils. The success of this and other groups led to the setting-up of nine regional partnerships with initial support from NAGTY and finance from DfES. Each partnership had a steering group composed of representatives from local authorities, higher education institutions, regional organisations concerned with gifted and talented children and NAGTY. Each regional partnership organised professional training; sought to support schools and areas in greatest need; tried to ensure that all 11- to 19-year-olds who fall into the top 5% of the ability range were registered with NAGTY; provided opportunities for practitioner research and arranged challenging activities for pupils. Under the YG&T Programme, nine Excellence Hubs have been created to continue and expand the work of the regional partnerships.

Every Child Matters: *Change for Children* and the Children Act 2004

The likelihood of all children reaching their potential has always been hampered by the fragmented nature of agencies concerned with provision for them. Vital information held by an agency about a child's needs has often been kept back from other agencies, including schools. This has had a particularly negative impact on the disadvantaged, for example, looked-after children. In 2004, 57% of looked-after children left school without even one GCSE or GNVQ and only 6% achieved five or more good GCSEs (see national statistics at www.dfes.gov.uk/rsgateway/). This represents a huge waste of national talent as well as many personal tragedies.

The Children Act 2004 sought to overcome these problems by, amongst other things, requiring:

- local authorities to make arrangements to promote cooperation between agencies to ensure the well-being of all children

- all children's services to bear these five outcomes in mind when planning provision. Children should:

  - be healthy

  - stay safe

  - enjoy and achieve

  - make a positive contribution

  - achieve economic well-being.

There are major implications for schools in seeking to achieve these outcomes for their most able pupils, especially where there is deprivation and/or low aspiration:

- local authorities to appoint a director of children's services to coordinate education and social services

- each local authority to take on the role of corporate parent to promote the educational achievement of looked-after children. This should help to ensure that greater consideration is given to their education when changes in foster placements are being considered

- the setting-up of an integrated inspection regime to look at the totality of provision for children.

More information can be found at www.everychildmatters.gov.uk.

Higher Standards, Better Schools for All (Education White Paper, October 2005)

Although the thrust of this Education White Paper is to improve educational opportunities for all, there is no doubt that some proposals will particularly benefit the most able, especially those that are disadvantaged in some way.

- Pupils receiving free school meals will be able to get **free public transport** to any one of three secondary schools closest to their homes between two and six miles away. At present, such children have very little choice in secondary schooling because their parents cannot afford the fares. This measure will allow them access to schools that might be better able to cater for their particular strengths and needs.

- **The National Register of Gifted and Talented Learners** will record the top 5% of the nation's children, as identified by a wide range of measures, so that they can be tracked and supported throughout their school careers. At first, the focus will be on 11- to 19-year-olds but later identification will start at the age of 4. As a first step, in 2006 all secondary schools were asked to identify gifted and talented students in the school census. In reality, some authorities had already begun this monitoring process but making it a national priority will bring other schools and authorities up to speed.

- In line with new school managerial structures, **'leading teachers' of the gifted and talented** will take the place of gifted and talented coordinators. Training (optionally accredited) will be organised through the national strategies. Leading teachers will work closely with School Improvement Partners and local authority coordinators to implement G&T improvement plans, and undertake much of the work previously undertaken by school coordinators.

- **Additional training** in providing for gifted and talented pupils will be available to all schools.

- **A national programme of non-residential summer schools** will be organised to run alongside gifted and talented summer schools already provided by local authorities and individual schools.

- Secondary schools will be encouraged to make greater use of **grouping by ability** in order to meet the needs of the most able and to use **curriculum flexibility** to allow pupils to take Key Stage 3 tests and GCSE courses early and to mix academic and vocational courses.

- **At advanced level, a new extended project** will allow the most able students to demonstrate high scholastic ability.

- **Extended schools** (see later section).

- **More personalised learning** (see later section).

More information on *Higher Standards, Better Schools for All* can be found at www.dfes.gov.uk/publications/schoolswhitepaper.

Extended schools

In many parts of the country, extended schools are already operating, but it is intended that schools will become much more central in providing a wide range of services to children, parents and the community. The government intends to spend £680 million by 2008 to facilitate these developments. Ideally these services should include:

- all-year childcare from 8.00am to 6.00pm

- referral to a wide range of support services, such as speech therapy, mental health and behaviour support

- exciting activities, including study support and extension/enrichment activities that will motivate the most able

- parenting support, which might include classes on healthy eating, helping children with homework, dealing with challenging behaviour, etc.

- community use of school facilities, especially ICT.

Again, this is an initiative that will benefit all children, especially those whose carers work. However, there are particular benefits for those children whose school performance suffers because they have nowhere to study at home and for those with talents that parents cannot nurture because of limited means.

More information on extended schools can be found at www.teachernet.gov.uk/settingup and www.tda.gov.uk/remodelling/extendedschools.aspx.

Personalised learning

As mentioned earlier in this chapter, a key component of current education reforms is the emphasis on personalised learning – maximising potential by tailoring education to individual needs, strengths and interests. The key features of personalised learning are:

- **Assessment for Learning** – Information from data and the tasks and assessments pupils undertake must be used to feed back suggestions about how work could be improved and what learning they need to do next. But the feedback should be a two-way process with pupils also providing information to teachers about factors impeding their learning and approaches that would enhance it. This feedback should inform future lesson planning. For the most able pupils, effective assessment for learning should mean that they move forward with their learning at an appropriate pace and depth, rather than marking time while others catch up.

- **Effective Teaching and Learning Strategies** – It is still the case that many teachers teach only in the way that was most successful for them as learners. There is ample evidence that our most able pupils do not form an homogeneous group and that, in order to bring out their many and varied gifts and talents, we need to adopt a wide range of teaching strategies, making full use of the opportunities provided by ICT. At the same time pupils need to become aware of the learning strategies that are most successful for them, whilst also exploring a broader range of learning approaches.

- **Curriculum Entitlement and Choice** – There are many examples of highly gifted adults whose abilities were masked at school because the curriculum did not appear to be relevant to them. Schools need to take the opportunities afforded by new flexibility in the curriculum, by the specialised diplomas of study being introduced for 14- to 19-year-olds and by partnership with other schools, colleges and businesses to engage their pupils. There are several schools now where more able pupils cover Key Stage 3 in two years. The year that is freed up by this approach can be used in a variety of ways, such as starting GCSE courses early, following an enrichment programme or taking up additional science and language courses. The possibilities are endless if there is desire for change.

- **School Organisation** – Effective personalisation demands a more flexible approach to school organisation. This flexibility might show itself in the way teaching and support staff are deployed, by the way pupils are grouped, by the structure of the school day and by the way in which ICT is used to enable learning to take place beyond the classroom. At least one school is abandoning grouping by age in favour of grouping by ability in the hope that this will provide the necessary challenge for the most able. It remains to be seen how successful this approach is but experimentation and risk-taking is essential if we are to make schooling relevant and exciting for our most able pupils.

- **Partnerships Beyond Schools** – Schools cannot provide adequately for their most able pupils without making full use of the opportunities and expertise offered by other groups within the community, including parents together with family support groups, social and health services, sports clubs and other recreational and business organisations.

The websites www.standards.dfes.gov.uk/personalisedlearning and www.teachernet. gov.uk/publications/ will provide more information on personalised learning, whilst new curriculum opportunities to be offered to 14- to 19-year-olds are described in www.dfes.gov.uk/14-19.

Self-evaluation and inspection

The most able must have as many opportunities for development as other pupils. Poor, unchallenging teaching or an ideology that confuses equality of opportunity with levelling down should not hinder their progress. They should have a fair share of a school's resources both in terms of learning materials and in human resources. The environment for learning should be one in which it is safe to be clever and to excel. These are points that schools should consider when preparing their self-evaluation and school development plans.

There have been dramatic changes in the relationships between schools and local authorities and in the schools' inspection regime since the Children Act 2004. Local authorities are now regarded as commissioners for services for children. One of their tasks is to facilitate the appointment of SIPs, School Improvement Partners, who act as the main conduit between schools and LAs and take part in an 'annual conversation' with their schools when the school's self-evaluation and progress towards targets is discussed.

Self-evaluation is also the cornerstone of the new shorter, more frequent Ofsted inspections, using a SEF (self-evaluation form) as a central point of reference together with the five outcomes for children of *Every Child Matters*. An invaluable tool for schools recognising that they need to do more for their gifted and talented pupils, or simply wanting to assess their current provision, is the institutional quality standards for gifted and talented education (IQS).

Institutional quality standards for gifted and talented education (IQS)

These standards, developed by a partnership of the DfES, NAGTY and other interested groups, are an essential self-evaluation tool for any school focusing on its gifted and talented provision. Under each of five headings, schools look carefully at the level indicators and decide which of the three levels they have achieved:

- **Entry level** – a school making its first steps towards developing a whole-school policy might find that much of its provision falls into this category. Ofsted would rate such provision satisfactory.

- **Developing level** – where there is some effective practice but there is room for development and improvement. This aligns with a good from Ofsted.

- **Exemplary level** – where good practice is exceptional and sustained. Ofsted would rate this excellent.

The five headings show clear links to the personalisation agenda: effective teaching and learning strategies; enabling curriculum entitlement and choice; assessment for learning; school organisation; and strong partnerships beyond school.

Having identified the levels at which they are performing, schools are then able to draw up development plans. A copy of these standards is included in the appendices and more information about them can be found at www2.teachernet. gov.uk/qualitystandards.

Resources for teachers and parents of more able pupils

There is currently an abundance of resources and support agencies for teachers, parents and gifted and talented young people themselves. A few of general interest are included below. Other geography examples will be found in later chapters of this book.

World Class Tests

These have been introduced by QCA to allow schools to judge the performance of their most able pupils against national and international standards. Currently tests are available for 9- and 13-year-olds in mathematics and problem solving. Some schools have found that the problem solving tests are effective at identifying able underachievers in maths and science. The website contains sample questions so that teachers, parents and pupils themselves can assess the tests' suitability for particular pupils or groups of pupils, and the tests themselves are also available online. For more information go to www. worldclassarena.org.uk.

National Curriculum Online

This website, administered by QCA, provides general guidance on all aspects of the National Curriculum but also has a substantial section on general and subject-specific issues relating to gifted and talented education, including identification strategies, case studies, management and units of work. Details of the National Curriculum Online can be found at www.nc.uk.net/gt.

G&TWise

G&TWise links to recommended resources for gifted and talented pupils, checked by professionally qualified subject editors, in all subjects and at all key stages and provides up-to-date information for teachers on gifted and talented education. Details can be found at www2.teachernet.gov.uk.

NACE – the National Association for Able Children in Education

NACE is an independent organisation that offers support for teachers and other professionals trying to develop provision for gifted and talented pupils. It gives advice and guidance to teachers and others, runs courses and conferences, provides consultants and keynote speakers.

It has also produced the NACE Challenge Award Framework, which it recommends could be used alongside IQS, as it exemplifies evidence and action planning. While IQS indicates what needs to be improved, the Challenge Award Framework suggests how to effect change. More information can be found at www.nace.co.uk.

National Association for Gifted Children (NAGC)

NAGC is a charity providing support for gifted and talented children and young people and their parents and teachers. It has a regional structure and in some parts of the country there are branch activities for children and parents. NAGC provides: counselling for both young people and their parents; INSET and courses for teachers; publications; activities for 3- to 10-year-olds; and a dedicated area on its website for 11- to 19-year-olds (to which they have exclusive access), called Youth Agency. For further information go to www. nagcbritain.org.uk.

Children of High Intelligence (CHI)

CHI acts on behalf of children whose intelligence puts them above the 98th percentile. It often acts in a support capacity when parents are negotiating appropriate provision with schools and local authorities. For further details visit www.chi-charity.org.uk.

Summary

- Schools must provide suitable challenge and support for their most able pupils.
- Appropriate provision can enhance motivation and improve behaviour.
- Recent legislation to support disadvantaged children should mean that fewer potentially gifted and talented children fall through the net.
- Effective self-evaluation of school provision for gifted and talented pupils and challenging targets are the keys to progress.
- There are many agencies that can help teachers with this work.

CHAPTER 2

Departmental policy and approach

- The role of the subject/department leader
- Responsibility for more able pupils
- Department policy
- Auditing current provision
- Collaborative learning, grouping policy and acceleration
- Allocating resources
- Monitoring and evaluation
- Liaison with other departments
- INSET activities

The purpose of this chapter is to suggest how a geography department can develop policies to ensure that there is effective provision for the most able. It looks at the responsibilities of the subject leader and suggests ways of putting policies for the most able in place.

The role of the subject/department leader

In 1998 the then DfES produced National Standards for subject leaders. Whilst not specifically part of the revised standards for 2007 they remind us of the obligations all subject leaders have in ensuring effective provision for the pupils in their charge. The extracts given below set out some of the obligations subject leaders must plan for and facilitate. The key messages, about personalising learning, from these extracts are:

- ensuring the curriculum meets the needs of all pupils, including the most able

- ensuring resources are provided, and new resources developed, to deliver the curriculum

- using targets to establish positive standards for pupils' achievement

- making use of continuing professional development (CPD) opportunities to develop staff confidence and competence in challenging more able pupils, and having expectations about the high quality of teaching required.

These standards present many challenges, not least of which is how best to provide for more able pupils. Geography is well placed as a subject to promote a broad range of learning opportunities and the development of skills but, to ensure that this becomes a reality, a policy of intent and some frameworks for implementation are required.

Extracts from the National Standards for subject leaders

Strategic direction and development of the subject

- Develop and implement policies and practices for the subject which reflect the school's commitment to high achievement, effective teaching and learning.

- Create a climate which enables other staff to develop and maintain positive attitudes towards the subject and confidence in teaching it.

Teaching and learning

- Ensure curriculum coverage, continuity and progression in the subject for all pupils, including those of high ability and those with special educational or linguistic needs.

- Provide guidance on the choice of appropriate teaching and learning methods to meet the needs of the subject and of different pupils.

- Set expectations and targets for staff and pupils in relation to standards of pupil achievement and the quality of teaching; establish clear targets for pupil achievement, and evaluate progress and achievement in the subject by all pupils, including those with special or linguistic needs.

Leading and managing staff

- Enable teachers to achieve expertise in their subject teaching.

- Ensure that the headteacher, senior managers and governors are well informed about subject policies, plans and priorities, success in meeting objectives and targets, and subject-related professional development plans.

Efficient and effective deployment of staff and resources

- Ensure the effective and efficient management and organisation of learning resources, including information and communications technology.

- Maintain existing resources and explore opportunities to develop or incorporate new resources from a wide range of sources inside and outside the school.

Effective departmental provision does not occur by chance. It is important that good practice in some classrooms is not being undermined by ineffective practice in others, and it is the responsibility of the subject leader to ensure that provision is consistently good in all geography classrooms. This can be a minefield and is exactly why a departmental policy is required. Consistent delivery and sharing best practice allow a department to become effective in its provision for more able pupils. In addition, departments need to audit their own practice, then to monitor and evaluate what they put in place.

Focus	Criteria for judgement at good or better
Teaching	• Teaching methods are imaginative and lead to high levels of interest from most pupils. • Individual needs are well catered for. • Teaching Assistants are well deployed to make a significant contribution to learning. • Adults relate well to pupils and expect them to work hard. • The level of challenge is realistic and pupils are productive. • Staff understand the next steps pupils need to take in their learning and they provide a wide range of activities to help them learn. • Homework is challenging.
Assessment	• Pupils are regularly involved in assessing their own work. • Assessment information is used well to establish challenging targets for all pupils. • Consistent and effective practices are in place for assessing work. • Assessment is used well to identify students who are under achieving and target intervention appropriately and effectively.
Progress	• The progress of the great majority of pupils is good in relation to their capacity and their prior attainment. • Work is appropriately challenging.
Learning	• Pupils' gains in knowledge, skills or understanding are high. • Pupils' consolidation in knowledge, skills or understanding is high. • The objectives set in the lesson are exceeded or objectives which set high expectations are achieved. • Expectations for the lesson are challenging and set high. • Work builds progressively on pupils' current knowledge, skills and understanding and proceeds at a good pace.
Pupil development	• Pupils are interested and absorbed in their work. • Most pupils are keen to achieve as well as they can. • Relationships are harmonious (teacher/pupil and pupil/pupil). • Pupils willingly accept responsibilities and carry them out well. • Pupils are willing to undertake work on their own accord/use their initiative. • Pupils behave well in the lesson. • Pupils attend class regularly. • Pupils feel secure. • Pupils are safety conscious.

Extracts from the Ofsted *Handbook for Inspecting Secondary Schools* (2003)

The criteria used by Ofsted when judging lessons are shown above. This is not presented as an inspection tool, but as an opportunity for a department to be more diagnostic about its provision, to examine current practice and to consider development needs. It can also be used as a framework for monitoring and evaluation. Using this as a framework can lead to focused discussion about curriculum change. Indeed, some schools have used this as a starting point for changing whole-school approaches to teaching and learning. Although the Ofsted framework for inspections changed in 2005 and individual subject departments are no longer inspected separately, it is important for teachers and subject leaders to think about what makes an effective lesson. In future, Ofsted inspectors are likely to look more closely at whole-school issues, such as provision for more able pupils across the curriculum.

The initial questions for the subject leader to consider are:

- What makes effective provision for more able students?

- How effective is current provision?

- What needs to be done to improve effectiveness further?

- How does a department know that progress is effective and successful?

So what is 'effective practice'? Leat (in Eyre and Lowe 2002) argues that effective provision for the more able pupils is based on five pedagogical principles:

- **challenge** – where pupils are provided with the opportunity to demonstrate what they can do in terms of thinking and doing related to high level concepts in both independent and collaborative learning

- **high quality talk** – where pupils are provided with the opportunity to develop more advanced communication skills using a wide range of media, including information and communications technology (ICT). They are also encouraged to develop leadership roles within collaborative tasks, presenting ideas through presentations or debate and demonstrating their powers of critical thinking and evaluation

- **transforming information** – where pupils are asked to take information and represent it in different styles and formats, thereby developing self-ownership of their work

- **purpose** – where pupils are shown that geography is relevant to their lives and that geography is useful and makes a contribution to society

- **metacognition** – where pupils think about 'how' they have learnt, as opposed to simply 'what', and how their learning in geography could be transferred into other curriculum areas. Metacognition is essential in order to raise achievement further.

Geography subject leaders could use these five principles as a starting point to evaluate their existing schemes of work and individual lessons. They could also be used when planning new schemes of work so that future provision becomes more effective. Chapter 4 provides many examples of how these principles can be integrated into schemes of work and put into practice in the classroom.

Responsibility for more able pupils

Many geography departments are small and it is usual for the subject leader to be responsible for provision for the most able, hopefully with the support of other members of the department. In larger departments it may be possible for a second member of the department to take the lead in this area. A possible job description for a colleague with responsibility for the most able is shown below. The person responsible for provision for the most able geographers, whether it is the subject leader or another member of the department, will need to work closely with the school coordinator for gifted and talented pupils.

Job description: Coordinator of geography provision for able, gifted and talented pupils

Reporting to: head of department and line manager

To discuss with subject leader and/or line manager the school philosophy on education for more able and what is understood by provision.

To identify how provision could be made more effective within the geography department.

Job description

To:

- exemplify effective provision for able, gifted and talented pupils in the classroom and beyond

- in consultation with the department team, to produce, develop, monitor, evaluate and refine a whole-school policy for meeting the needs of able, gifted and talented pupils

- lead the implementation of the geography policy, supported by the subject leader, senior managers and governors

- work with department and subject managers to ensure a suitably differentiated and challenging curriculum of opportunity

- make a wide range of learning opportunities available to pupils, within and beyond the classroom

- manage the development of resources

- monitor the overall progress made by able, gifted and talented pupils

- manage the support of staff and the dissemination of effective practice

- ensure that provision for able, gifted and talented pupils is kept at the heart of the geography department's agenda for developing learning and teaching

- work with the school's manager of CPD to ensure that staff receive suitable training and development in identification and provision, organising and leading CPD

- keep up-to-date with current thinking and major initiatives. Network with other coordinators and maintain contact with national organisations such as NACE and the Geographical Association

- consult with staff at all levels and ensure the effective exchange of information within school and with other schools, particularly for transfer and transition from Key Stage 2.

The subject leader, or nominated representative for the more able pupils, is responsible for drawing up policies and translating them into accessible and usable schemes of work, supported by appropriate resources that will challenge the most able pupils. The outcomes should be evaluated to ensure that provision is effective, and changes undertaken as necessary. Although this may be the responsibility of one person, it is important that all those who teach geography are involved in discussions and planning. A collaborative approach to policy design will help to achieve collective ownership, which is key to the success of any policy being introduced.

Department policy

It is important that departmental policies are closely linked to the main aims and philosophy of the school, and that both school and departmental policies make it clear that provision for more able pupils is an entitlement. Eyre (1997) asserts that there are a number of reasons why policies for the more able are needed, including the goal of raising standards, the importance of ensuring inclusion and the need to encourage pupils to learn 'how to learn' as part of their personal development. Able pupils must not be allowed to underachieve and Eyre states that 'differentiation must be a departmental priority'.

The geography department policy should follow the same framework as the school policy for the more able and should fit in with its general philosophy. A good policy will develop from consultation with senior management, the gifted and talented coordinator, and other staff in the department. Below is an example of a whole-school policy, framed as a statement of intent.

Bramcote Hills Comprehensive School's draft policy statement for able children

A guiding statement of intent

- The governors and staff at Bramcote Hills Comprehensive School believe that support for the able helps all pupils to achieve their potential and seek to provide opportunities for this to happen.

- We believe that supporting the needs of the able pupils is a factor in raising achievement for all.

- We acknowledge that some children may have a talent in one area of the curriculum rather than an all-round ability.

- We acknowledge that some children have an ability which is so exceptional compared with their peer group that they may need special consideration in order to meet their needs.

- We believe that identification and provision are integral and are therefore actively pursuing developments in these areas to provide opportunities for all children to reveal, display and extend their abilities.

- We believe that the needs of all children are served best when the school works in an open, responsive and realistic partnership with parents.

As a starting point for preparing a departmental policy the following headings might be useful:

1. **Policy rationale and aims**

   - How does the policy relate to the school's overall aims and values?

   - How does the subject contribute to the young person's academic and personal development?

   - What does the department aim to provide for the most able pupils?

2. **Definitions**

   - In the context of your school and subject what do you mean by the most able or gifted and talented?

3. **Identification**

   - How does your department's approach fit in with the school's practice on identification?

   - What subject-specific identification strategies will you use?

4. **Organisational issues**

   - How will teaching groups be organised to meet the needs of all pupils including the most able?

   - Will fast tracking, early entry or acceleration to an older age group be considered and what measures will be taken both to support these pupils and to ensure that they continue to make progress?

5. **Provision in lessons**

   - How do schemes of work and lesson plans reflect demands to be made of the more able pupils?

   - How will the need for faster pace, more breadth and greater depth in the subject be met?

   - How are the thinking skills needed for this subject to be developed?

   - How will different learning styles of pupils be catered for?

   - How will homework and independent learning be used to enhance their education?

   - How is assessment, both formative and summative, used to enable suitable targets to be set and appropriate progress to be made?

   - Is Assessment for Learning (AfL) a core focus of departmental provision?

- How does the learning climate within the classroom support and encourage the most able, particularly with regard to reward and incentives?

6. Out-of-class activities

- What activities beyond the classroom might be arranged?
- How will study support for the more able be implemented?
- What collaboration with outside agencies is envisaged?

7. Transfer and transition

- How is information from primary schools used to ensure progression?
- What measures are taken to assist the most able pupils during their transition from primary to secondary school?
- How are pupils who move on to sixth forms in other schools or colleges supported?

8. Resources

- How are teaching assistants, learning mentors and other adult helpers used to support the more able?
- What outside agencies are used?
- What specific learning resources are available for the more able?
- How is ICT used to enhance the education of the more able?

9. Monitoring and evaluation

- Who is responsible for liaising with the school coordinator and developing good practice for the more able in your department?
- How is the effectiveness of this policy to be measured?
- What targets does the department have for its more able pupils (e.g. Levels 7 and 8 at Key Stage 3, A* and A at GCSE)?
- How and when is the progress of individual pupils and groups monitored?
- What continuing professional development (CPD) is needed or will be provided for colleagues?

10. Recognition and reward

- How will pupil and teacher success be recognised and rewarded?

An example is provided opposite of a departmental policy which could be amended to suit other schools. It includes most but not all of the above guidelines, which are suggested as a framework for policy design rather than as an absolute list of inclusions.

Geography department policy for more able pupils

Policy rationale and aims

The school aims to provide a stimulating education within a supportive and caring community. As a department, we are committed to providing an environment where all pupils including the most able can maximise their potential.

Criteria used for identification of gifted geographers

A student gifted in geography will demonstrate many of these characteristics:

- have a real enthusiasm for geography, impressive geographical knowledge and a genuine interest in the world around them

- write clearly, incorporating data and showing high levels of reasoning, argument and logical thinking

- have well-considered opinions on a range of issues and can appreciate the values and attitudes of others

- show an ability to transfer knowledge, understanding and skills between subjects and to new situations

- enjoy using visual methods to present and interpret data such as graphs, charts, maps, photographs, satellite images and weather maps

- have a high degree of spatial awareness which may be shown through interpretation of maps and diagrams

- be confident and contribute effectively when taking part in less formal teaching situations such as discussion, role play or fieldwork.

Identification should be by looking at the quality of written work in lessons, including assessments. Open-ended tasks are likely to be a good indicator as is ability to take part in discussion and to express their own viewpoint but also to take account of other ideas. Pupils' attitude to lessons and to their work in general is also important.

Strategies

Subject teachers should look for opportunities for extension and enrichment for the most able. Some useful approaches are:

- to encourage independent research

- to ask more challenging questions and expect fuller, well reasoned answers

- to set open-ended tasks

- to have higher expectations for the quality of work

- to ensure students know how to achieve their fullest potential by using a range of AfL (Assessment for Learning) strategies

- to differentiate resources or produce additional resources where appropriate

- to expect the more able to work more quickly

- to encourage participation in out-of-class activities

- to recognise and praise achievement.

Monitoring and evaluation

Pupils identified as gifted geographers must be listed in the departmental gifted and talented register. All subject teachers must keep a record in their mark book or planner. At the end of each school year the progress of these pupils will be discussed at a department meeting and information about each student will be passed on to the person who will be teaching them the following year.

It is the head of department's responsibility to liaise with the school gifted and talented coordinator.

Auditing current provision

A thorough and honest audit of existing provision and levels of achievement of the most able is important. From this, the development priorities and an action plan can be developed. Appendices 2.1, 2.2 and 2.3 show three alternative checklists which could be used to audit provision for the most able. Copies of these are also available on the website. Appendix 2.1 is a selection of focus questions which could be used to initiate departmental discussion and to identify priorities for development. Appendix 2.2 is an alternative checklist based on Leat's five pedagogical principles for effective provision (Leat 1998). Appendix 2.3 illustrates how assessment provision could be audited against a range of learning tools. Both Appendices 2.2 and 2.3 are focused on Key Stage 3 but could easily be adapted for other key stages.

Once the auditing process is complete, the subject leader and team can construct an action plan, prioritising future developments. A template for such action priorities is provided in Appendix 2.4.

Collaborative learning, grouping policy and acceleration

Collaborative learning and grouping policy

It is clear that the more able pupils need to be encouraged to take on a variety of activities to extend, enrich and accelerate their learning, and class teachers should facilitate this. High quality talk is one of the key areas where higher learning achievement is possible, so management of talk needs careful consideration and planning. Group work can give more able pupils the opportunity to:

- develop leadership skills
- develop high order questioning skills
- mentor the learning of other pupils
- articulate their information processing and reasoning skills.

Collaborative learning has many advantages, but teachers need to consider the structure of groups and how different group compositions might affect learning. Strategies which could promote greater development for more able pupils include:

- the **structured mix**, which allows the more able pupils to shine in a carefully managed leadership capacity

- the **random mix**, which can allow more able pupils to develop their ability to model ideas and mentor other pupils

- **ability groups**, which may allow more able pupils to demonstrate high quality knowledge and skills, although not necessarily providing other opportunities that they might benefit from. With this arrangement, other pupils within a class could miss out because they will be deprived of contributions from the most able

- **friendship groups**, which sometimes encourage good collaborative work but may give pupils the opportunity to drift.

The structured mix, therefore, is often the most effective group composition for more able pupils.

The size of group is also important and some of the benefits and limitations of different sized groups are listed.

Size	Benefits	Limitations	When to use
Individual	• student has to think independently	• inability to share own experience and knowledge	• where original work is required
Pair	• student is obliged to converse • unthreatening and secure experience • quick and practical	• conversation may end too quickly, not promoting high quality talk • little challenge with views, values and attitudes	• where brief discussion is required • where topic content is sensitive
Small group 3–4	• diversity of opinion • pairs can be collapsed into groups of four	• some students may stay quiet • scope for social pressures	• confidence building • staged discussion before whole-class activity • increases social interaction within a class

Size	Benefits	Limitations	When to use
Large group 5–7	• diversity of ideas and opinion • builds confidence in contributing to whole-class discussions	• requires chairing and social skills, a good opportunity for the more able student • individuals can dominate • some students can remain quiet	• developing teamwork opportunities • where a wide range of views, ideas, attitudes need to be covered • where the topic invites the idea of assuming roles
Whole class	• an equal experience for all • teacher can support/direct the conversation	• many students cannot remain quiet • more able students can overdominate • there can be frustration from waiting time in order to contribute	• where students need to hear the same information

Group size considerations (from *Literacy in Geography,* Standards and Effectiveness Unit – Speaking and Listening Workshop, © Crown Copyright 2001)

Acceleration

Some schools, particularly but not exclusively those which are independent, have chosen to move the more able pupils through the academic route more quickly, by creating a fast track or accelerated group. Clearly, this must be part of a whole-school strategic plan with the agreement of staff, governors and parents. For example, in some schools Key Stage 3 delivery is compressed into two years, with GCSE courses starting in Year 9. This means that pupils take some GCSEs in Year 10 and can create time for the early start of AS level or for additional complementary courses in Year 11. This might include the introduction of geology or environmental science which would build on and extend geographical knowledge and skills.

Acceleration checklist

Acceleration means:

• early entry

• year hopping

• telescoping – a set amount of work covered by a select group of pupils, covered in a short period of time

• compacting

- subject acceleration
- in-class acceleration
- vertical grouping – teaching children of different ages together.

Benefits of acceleration:

- improves confidence, motivation and scholarship
- helps prevent the development or habit of mental laziness
- helps to avoid underachievement and boredom
- reduces egotism and arrogance
- gives positive attitudes towards learning
- allows for early completion of education.

Considerations before acceleration:

- gaining parental agreement and support
- child's readiness for it socially, emotionally, physically
- child's readiness to be separated from friends
- is attainment high for age?
- seeking a second opinion, e.g. from an educational psychologist
- anxiety and stress level, perseverance
- impact on other children in family

From George, D. (2003) *Gifted Education Identification and Provision*. David Fulton Publishers, p. 68.

The acceleration checklist given shows that the advantages of this approach include improved confidence and motivation, and reduced underachievement and boredom. It might also have the potential to improve external examination results. However, for many schools this is not a suitable option, particularly where the range of ability is wide.

Allocating resources

Clearly there are resource implications for departments trying to improve their provision for the most able. On the other hand, there is unlikely to be funding within the annual department budget which is specifically allocated to providing for the most able, and most budget holders would not want this type of limitation. However, this is not to say that the spending of the annual budget does not need to be mindful of the needs of all pupils, including the most able. Subject leaders should also be proactive in exploring other avenues for funding developments for the most able. Schools may have funds within their budget for gifted and talented initiatives; alternatively funding may be secured from school development allocation in schools with specialist designation. Of course, there are many other resources which departments can and should use in addition to money. Some of these are shown in the diagram below.

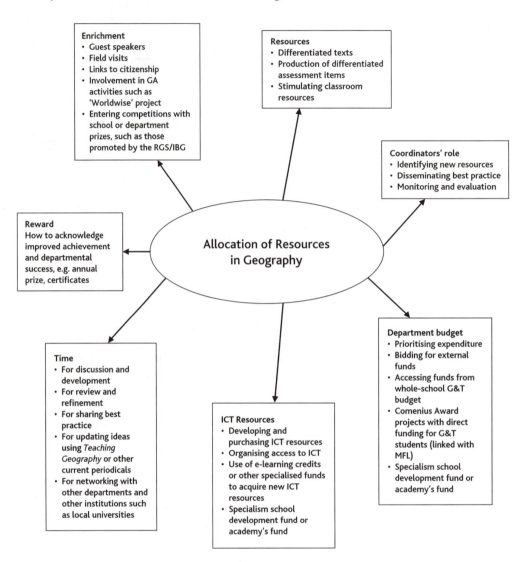

Monitoring and evaluation

It is important to make sure that effective strategies to monitor and evaluate the measures taken are put in place. Monitoring requires collecting information about how provision is being delivered by members of the department, particularly provision for the most able and the tasks they are asked to do. Appendix 2.5 shows a lesson observation schedule with G&T focus; Appendix 2.6 provides a form which could be used for obtaining student work analysis feedback.

Having looked at this evidence, it will also be necessary to evaluate the schemes of work, in order to make sure that these clearly indicate the strategies which are expected to provide challenge for the most able. A form for obtaining scheme of work feedback is given in Appendix 2.7.

Each of these monitoring and evaluation frameworks could be adapted to suit particular circumstances.

A policy for the more able should also give pupils responsibility for recognising their own achievements. To facilitate this, Appendix 2.8 shows a pupil record card designed by the Minster School, Southwell, Nottinghamshire, to encourage pupils to reflect on their achievements and to comment on their success. They are also encouraged to set themselves targets showing how they think they can improve. Pupils keep this card as part of a portfolio of evidence, and it is one part of the evidence used when assigning National Curriculum Levels at the end of the year or Key Stage.

Appendix 2.9 provides a framework for reporting back to a department team or line manager about the quality of standards in terms of strengths and areas for further development. This forms the evaluation document and it is essential that all members of a department team are aware of, and understand, the process. The evaluation report should act as a starting point for renewed discussion and development to continue the journey of improving geography provision for the more able.

Liaison with other departments

Isolated provision has never been, and never will be, fully effective: collaboration is vital in order to share best practice and to move provision for more able pupils forward. Collaboration allows departments which have good ideas to discuss some of their strategies with others. This can provide mutual support and encouragement between departments. The case studies below provide examples of how geography teams have worked in partnership with other areas of the school curriculum for mutual support and subject delivery.

- Geography and modern foreign language departments reinforce the concept of weather observations and recording, by planning to deliver the topic at the same time.

- Geography works with the social studies department to promote and display effective strategies for revision. This could include organising pupils into 'learning circles' outside the classroom, which encourage revision to be more active and help to raise confidence before examinations.

- Geography, religious education and music departments work together with Year 7 classes, leading to presentations on cultural diversity. Each subject area provides expert input, encouraging high quality presentations. This has the potential to become a year group competition as well as an assessment.

- Geography and ICT. Pupils are asked to research and present a newspaper report on a recent hazard event of their choice, focusing on cause and effect. The geography department provides expertise about natural hazards, and the technical skills of effective web research and newspaper publication are delivered by the ICT team. This also helps to overcome problems of access to ICT facilities.

- Departments involved with work-related learning collaborate to design an information leaflet for pupils, showing how their subjects are relevant to the world of work. This is used to promote uptake of the subjects for GCSE.

INSET activities

In addition to collaboration within the department, whole-school INSET activities can also provide a platform for sharing ideas about effective provision for more able pupils. This builds on the concept that collaboration is the best way to ensure consistency and to acknowledge and share success. The examples below illustrate whole-school INSET activities where geography has made a key input, and shows that a school's most valuable resource is its staff and that external providers are not always required:

- The Lending in Learning project in Nottinghamshire is involved with developing and trialling differentiated and collaborative teaching and learning techniques to raise standards and improve pupil motivation. In a school involved with this programme, the geography department was one of the subject areas involved, promoting the use of inductive learning and thinking skills. The department presented workshops as part of a whole-school Teaching and Learning INSET event. Classroom ideas were shared between subject areas and a cross-curricular Improving Learning group was established to introduce and embed Assessment for Learning approaches across the curriculum.

- A school geography department has formed a partnership with Nottingham University to develop 'Fantastic Geographies'. These are geographical themes which could be included at Key Stage 3 to motivate pupils and promote interest in the subject. Recent examples of new schemes of work which have been devised by new entrants to the profession include: the Geography of World Hunger, the Geography of Conflict and the Geography of Christmas.

Fantastic Geographies

An extract from the PGCE Method Course, University of Nottingham

Context

Concern has been expressed in the academic literature and in the media over the 'fossilisation' of the content of the school geography curriculum, and the issue of the increasing gap between university and school geography is part of this discussion. There is a complex and detailed history both to the conception of the geography school curriculum and to this discussion. The introduction of a university method session on 'Fantastic Geographies' aimed both to alert students and teachers to this ongoing debate and concern and to enable them to consider how their own understanding of geography, based on their geography courses, might impact on the school geography curriculum.

Key questions to consider

- In what ways has the content of the geography schemes of work at KS3 changed in the last five years?
- Similarly, how has the geography content taught in terms of the GCSE and A level specifications changed in recent years?
- How have recent curriculum initiatives such as Citizenship Education and Education for Sustainable Development impacted upon changes in the geography content?
- What other factors are responsible for these changes?
- How does the geography department manage change in geography content within their schemes of work?
- What are the issues the department faces in implementing such changes?

Task

To consider the issues raised in the above questions whilst in school. To assist the department, by the development of a new Fantastic Geography scheme of work, to emphasise skill development, research and relevance in a modern geography curriculum.

Source: University of Nottingham *PGCE Course Handbook* (Mary Biddulph)

Summary

- Subject leaders must be aware of their obligations with regard to the more able students in their subject area.
- Subject leaders must be confident about what constitutes effective provision for the more able pupils and how this can be facilitated in the classroom.
- Assessment for Learning, the application of Thinking Skills and the use of ICT are all appropriate vehicles for challenging and supporting achievement for the most able.
- Auditing current provision for the more able students highlights effective best practice and identifies 'gaps'. This forms the basis for focused discussion and action planning.
- A collaborative approach to devising departmental policy is important.
- There is a range of resource and funding opportunities.
- Subject leaders must be confident about their approaches to monitoring and evaluation, in line with the whole-school policy.
- Liaison between school departments can bring significant benefits.

CHAPTER 3

Recognising high ability and potential

- Recognising and identifying the most able geographers
- Multiple intelligences
- Creativity and geography: Renzulli's three-ring model of giftedness

The purpose of this chapter is to explore the characteristics of pupils who are very able in geography, so that they can be recognised in the classroom and given appropriate learning opportunities and support to fulfil their potential.

Geography is unique in that it links together other subjects, combining knowledge from both the arts and the sciences to deepen our understanding of the world around us. To use the analogy of different subjects as overlapping Olympic rings, Geography is the ring that fringes on and binds together all the others, with the focus on geography as being concerned with space and place. This linking of, and across, different subjects is, of course, geography's great strength in the school curriculum, giving pupils a perspective on learning, in terms of knowledge, understanding and skills, that few other subjects can match. Combined with this is the fact that geography is highly topical and relevant to the everyday world around us and, when taught well, is stimulating and fascinating in equal measure. For our pupils, in terms of teaching and learning, geography

> draws upon information in many forms – text, image, moving image, symbols, graphics, spoken word, models and sound . . . it can appeal to all the senses and use the spectrum of cognitive and emotional processes that help make sense of rich information.
>
> (Eyre and Lowe 2002)

Clearly these processes are highly developed in our most able geographers, and it is worth looking in some detail at who these pupils are and how we can identify them.

Recognising and identifying the most able geographers

Geography tends not to produce the child prodigy – unlike, say, mathematics or music. Furthermore, it is unusual for a pupil to be identified as an exceptionally able geographer by a primary school even by the time of transfer to secondary school. This is partly because the subject requires a degree of maturity and perspective, but also because there are few geography specialists in the primary sector and, in many primary schools, very little time is allocated to geography. In January 2004, the Chief Inspector of Schools reported on the relative neglect of certain subjects in primary schools, including geography, as a result of the focus in recent years on the National Literacy and Numeracy Strategies. However, there clearly are outstanding young geographers coming from primary school who should be identified early in Year 7.

Case study – Early excellence: Year 7 pupil already working at Level 7

Mary achieved Level 7 on her first levelled assessment in secondary school. In both her oral and written work, she shows clear and creative thinking and is able to make connections between different concepts and areas of study. Her teacher uses open-ended thinking skills tasks and more advanced GCSE texts where appropriate to extend her learning.

Some possible methods of identification of exceptional ability in geography are:

- analysis of data, e.g. Key Stage 3 National Curriculum tests, CATs, VRs, NVRs

- MidYIS/YELLIS/ALPS data

- primary school information

- teacher assessments

- students' work

- classroom observation, e.g. discussion, debating and presentation skills

- discussions with students.

Each geography department and school will make its own decisions about the amount and type of data used. Lesson observations and professional judgements about what pupils achieve and contribute in lessons are no less significant than numbers and assessments. It is clearly important to discuss with others the qualities observed in particularly able geographers. It is also important to remember that there can be significant changes in such qualities in pupils; for example, when incoming Year 7s experience Key Stage 3 work for the first time, or with progression from Key Stage 3 to Key Stage 4. There may also be significant developments in pupils' abilities over the summer period between Years 6 and 7, particularly for those participating in transition activities such as summer school (see Chapter 6).

In many secondary schools, the most able geographers will not always be identified by the criteria used by the whole-school gifted and talented coordinator. It is important that the geography department ensures that particularly able geographers find their way onto the school register of more able students, because this recognition may offer pupils the chance to participate in a variety of extracurricular extension and enrichment opportunities. It is also important for class teachers to know which pupils are particularly able, so that they can modify their teaching to provide the necessary challenge.

Curriculum guidelines for gifted and talented pupils in geography from QCA

Pupils who are considered gifted in geography are likely to be able to:

- **understand concepts clearly so that they can apply this understanding to new situations in order to make interpretations, develop hypotheses, reach conclusions and explore solutions**
They understand geographical ideas and theories, and apply them to real situations.

- **communicate effectively using both the written and spoken word**
They communicate knowledge, ideas and understanding in ways that are appropriate to the task and to the audience (for example, writing formal letters and reports, producing brochures representing particular groups). They learn subject-specific vocabulary, use it accurately and are able to define words.

- **reason, argue and think logically, showing an ability to manipulate abstract symbols and recognise patterns and sequences**
They use and apply mathematical principles (such as area, shape, spatial distribution) and formulae (such as Spearman's rank correlation coefficient) to solve geographical tasks and problems. They identify their own geographical questions and establish sequences of investigation. They understand, and are able to explain, complex processes and interrelationships (for example, within and between physical and human environments).

- **enjoy using graphs, charts, maps, diagrams and other visual methods to present information**
They transform relief shown by contour lines into three-dimensional models in their minds. They are competent and confident in using the wide range of visual resources required in geography – aerial photographs, satellite images, maps of different types and scales, GIS systems and so on.

- **be confident and contribute effectively when taking part in less formal teaching situations**
They take part readily in role-play situations or simulations and enjoy contributing to outdoor fieldwork.

- **relate well to other people, showing an ability to lead, manage and influence others, appreciating and understanding others' views, attitudes and feelings**
They are willing to share their knowledge and understanding and can steer discussion.

- **have a more highly developed value system than most pupils of their age**
They have well considered opinions on issues such as the environment and the inequalities of life in different places.

- **have a wide-ranging general knowledge about the world**
  They have good knowledge of where places are in the world and of topical issues.

- **be able to transfer knowledge from one subject to another**
  They transfer their knowledge of physics, for example, to understanding climate. Or they transfer knowledge of the industrial revolution from history to help explain the location of industry in the UK.

- **be creative and original in their thinking, frequently going beyond the obvious solution to a problem**
  For example, if faced with the problem of storm pipes being unable to cope with sudden storm surges in an area, they might suggest taking measures like afforestation to reduce storm surges, rather than proposing technical improvements to the pipe system. If faced with the problem of congested roads, they might suggest taxing cars more heavily, improving public transport or changing land use patterns, rather than building bigger roads.

Source: www.nc.uk.net/gt/geography/index.htm

These curriculum guidelines for gifted and talented in geography, taken from the Qualifications and Curriculum Authority (QCA) website, provide a useful starting point for the identification of able geographers, although pupils would not be expected to show all the listed characteristics. Sometimes it will be the relative strength and significance of individual qualities rather than the number of ticks on the list which is important. In a subject as all-encompassing as geography, it may also be possible for pupils to be stronger in some areas than in others – for example, to find geomorphology more interesting than population studies, or to be skilled at interpreting data but less good at contributing to class discussion or role play. Appendix 3.1 is a sheet which can be used to cross-reference the QCA guidelines to individual pupils.

Case study – Uneven performance: Year 9 pupil working at Level 6/7

Robert is highly focused when analysing data, for example development statistics, and is particularly skilled at creative and extended writing, where he sequences and links information very effectively. He is less confident and outstanding on more traditional methods of presentation, such as annotating diagrams, and needs more open-ended tasks to show off his best.

Case study – Values: Year 9 pupil working at Level 8

Rachel has consistently attained highly throughout Key Stage 3 and is aware of how geographic issues impact on the lives of people. She has a more highly developed values system than others in the class and relishes opportunities to promote awareness of global issues, e.g. organising a Fairtrade café on open evenings, and leading a 'One World' assembly focusing on a development project in Ghana with which the school has a link.

Using National Curriculum Levels to identify the most able

Consistently high performance in assessed work in geography is also likely to contribute to the identification of particularly able pupils. Most teachers are well aware of the limitations of the National Curriculum (NC) Levels and realise that high ability will show itself in ways beyond these descriptors and in forms that cannot always be easily assessed with a test or mark score. The NC Levels can, however, help to promote discussion and give geography departments some evidence on which to make judgements and to see where a pupil's performance is, compared with national standards.

Level 7 attainment target for Key Stage 3 geography

Pupils show their knowledge, skills and understanding in studies of a wide range of places and environments at various scales, from local to global, and in different parts of the world. They describe interactions within and between physical and human processes, and show how these interactions create geographical patterns and help change places and environments. They understand that many factors, including people's values and attitudes, influence the decisions made about places and environments, and use this understanding to explain the resulting changes. They appreciate that the environment in a place and the lives of the people who live there are affected by actions and events in other places. They recognise that human actions, including their own, may have unintended environmental consequences and that change sometimes leads to conflict. They appreciate that considerations of sustainable development affect the planning and management of environments and resources. With growing independence, they draw on their knowledge and understanding to identify geographical questions and issues and establish their own sequence of investigation. They select and use accurately a wide range of skills from the Key Stage 3 programme of study. They evaluate critically sources of evidence, present well-argued summaries of their investigations and begin to reach substantiated conclusions.

From *Geography: The National Curriculum for England* (1999) DfEE

A rapid checklist for identifying more able pupils in geography is given in Appendix 3.2. This list could also be used by departments as a basis for discussing individual pupils across all years, as it brings in a wide range of qualities in addition to those related to subject content and skills.

For geography departments to identify their most able pupils, the following questions are crucial:

- What does it mean to be very able in geography?

- What do we want an able geographer to be capable of doing?

- What constitutes excellence in geography at Key Stage 3, GCSE and post-16?

- Does the teaching of geography in the school allow excellence to flourish?

The last point is vital, since appropriate teaching provision and opportunities for able pupils is not just an outcome of identification but is an essential contributory factor to accurate identification. Put simply, the better one gets at identifying able geographers, the more confident one becomes at knowing what they can and should be doing. With more enriched and extended learning opportunities, other qualities in pupils may be identified and perhaps new and hitherto hidden able pupils may also be identified. This interdependence of identification and provision is shown diagrammatically below. Central to this model is the idea that neither provision nor identification is an end in itself, and thus it is important to develop challenging teaching and learning strategies that get pupils to aim high and look ahead at the implications and consequences of what they are currently studying.

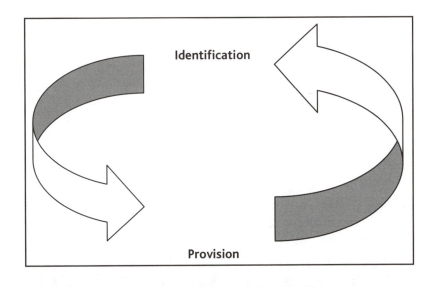

Identification

Provision

Case study – Going further: Year 8 pupil working at Level 7

Daniel's strengths were identified through project work. He has excellent research and ICT skills and uses both of these to good effect to show independence in his work. He regularly produces work that is very thorough and goes much further in his thinking and coverage than is asked for, or expected. He explores wider and more complex implications of geographic issues and responds particularly well to more open-ended tasks.

Identifying potential

Relying only on identification of pupils in Year 7 or 8 (as they enter secondary school) has some important disadvantages because some pupils will develop their abilities only as they become a little older. Sometimes, the requirements of schemes of work and exam courses do not bring out the best in more able pupils and it is only later in their school career, when they are given more extended opportunities to develop and explore their opinions and ideas, that they show their full potential.

Case study – Later excellence: Year 13 pupil achieving A grade at A level

Although sharp and able, Duncan achieved only moderately across his GCSEs and his entry to the sixth form was at first in some doubt. During his geography GCSE course, although interested and attentive in lessons, his written answers were often thin and underdeveloped. At AS and A Level however, he responded well to a range of geography topics and enjoyed the opportunity of developing his viewpoints and backing them up with evidence. He developed excellent questioning and discussion skills and his written work became thoughtful and incisive. Duncan developed into a mature student of a high calibre, achieving a top grade at A Level.

It is worth remembering that the few highest achievers in a geography assessment or piece of written work, with factually correct and well developed answers, may not be the only very able pupils in the class. There may also be pupils with acute discussion skills, original ideas and perceptive observation in the field, who cannot, or do not, show this in written form. An enriched and varied learning environment offers a better opportunity to ensure that high ability in geography is not missed; it may also help to identify pupils with potential, as well as those who are already demonstrating their ability.

Case study – Poor writing skills: Year 9 pupil, capable of Level 6/7 work

David is verbally precocious in class discussion, making sharply observed points and both answering and asking questions accurately. He is creative with his thinking, but poor handwriting skills hamper his ability to transfer this quality to his exercise book and his confidence suffers as a result. The teacher helps the situation by ensuring that David always uses his glossary of geographic terminology, using writing frames and by giving him choices in how he presents his information, e.g. more visual displays and a radio broadcast.

Case study – Pointing the way: Year 8 pupil working at Level 7

Shazia is an able and hardworking pupil who prefers to complete most of her work in her own time. She has found some of the more advanced and complicated concepts quite difficult but, through short and focused conversations with the teacher in lessons, she has been able to extend the breadth and depth of her project work by using a greater range of resource materials including websites and textbooks. She is now linking together ideas and seeing interrelationships in sophisticated and complex ways, e.g. considering how human actions might affect physical processes and the surrounding environment, which might in turn lead to conflict between different groups of people.

Geography departments also need to remember that some able pupils, perhaps those who are able in many subjects, can be under considerable pressure and can develop strategies to hide their true ability, or they may simply prioritise things other than geography.

Case study – Under pressure: Year 11 pupil, expected to gain an A*

Beth is very able across all her 12 GCSE subjects and should be on target to attain all As and A*s. She has a range of other interests inside and outside school and is finding it difficult to balance these with her heavy workload, particularly the demands of coursework. Normally sharp and thorough with her geography, recent written pieces have been more moderate, lacking the detail and flair her teacher is expecting.

Differentiating performance in geography

Peter Davies (1995) developed the idea of three overarching criteria which help differentiate performance in geography and therefore provide an additional strategy for identifying the most able.

- **Specificity**: this describes the ability of pupils to handle variables. Highly able geographers are able to handle complex variables relating to real-world situations and to understand the relationships between these variables. In describing and explaining, for example, climatic distributions, they would identify local as well as continental patterns; or, in using a choropleth map, they would be thinking in terms of several categories of shading, not just two or three.

- **Completeness**: this refers to the quality of explanations of links between variables. Highly able geographers would not make simple links between two sets of data but would identify other factors and think about interrelationships.

- **Judgement**: highly able students have an understanding of the complexity of most geographical issues in the world around us and are less likely to see things in terms of black and white, or to make sweeping statements or judgements as a result.

Another generic list, provided by George (2003), draws a distinction between the 'bright' child and the 'gifted' child (or the able and the exceptionally able). This list, shown on page 42, could be useful in differentiating between high achieving pupils. For example, the pupil who argues from the point of view of a member of Greenpeace in favour of nuclear power (to combat rapid global warming from burning fossil fuels) could be indicating critical and independent thinking; someone else, on the same issue, may be absorbing the complexity of the causes of the 'greenhouse effect', asking difficult questions about its validity and suggesting creative options for the future. Once again, providing appropriately challenging learning opportunities can draw out these characteristics and help in identification.

Differentiating between the 'bright' and the 'gifted' child

Bright child	Gifted child
Is interested	Is highly curious
Answers the questions	Discusses in detail
Knows the answers	Asks the questions
Is in a top set	Looks beyond the group
Grasps the meaning	Draws inferences
Is alert	Is keenly observant
Completes the work	Initiates projects
Has good ideas	Has unusual and silly ideas!
Enjoys school	Enjoys learning
Has a good memory	Is a good guesser
Is pleased with learning	Is highly critical
Is receptive	Is intense
Learns easily	Already knows
Enjoys straightforward sequential presentation	Thrives on complexity
Enjoys peers	Prefers adults or older pupils
Absorbs information	Manipulates information

(from George, D. (2003) *Gifted Education Identification and Provision.* David Fulton Publishers, p. 13.)

Multiple intelligences

The work of Howard Gardner (*Frames of Mind: the Theory of Multiple Intelligences* 1993, *Intelligence Reframed: Multiple Intelligences for the 21st Century* 1999) changed the view of the nature of intelligence. The types of intelligence he identified are listed below, and able students may have a marked preference for one or more of these styles. Identification of able pupils and subsequent provision by teachers should take account of these preferences.

Howard Gardner's multiple intelligences

- **Verbal/Linguistic**: those with a good command of language and words
- **Logical/Mathematical**: the puzzle solvers
- **Visual/Spatial**: those who can easily translate space and dimension
- **Bodily/Kinaesthetic**: those with a good brain–body connection
- **Musical/Rhythmic**: those with a natural flair for music, rhythm and dance
- **Interpersonal**: the team players, good with people
- **Intrapersonal**: the reflective and more philosophical people
- **Naturalistic**: those who recognise patterns in and make connections to elements in nature.

A useful and succinct way of incorporating Gardner's work is (to paraphrase the question that he posed) not to consider a class of pupils and say, 'How able are they in geography?' but to ask instead, 'How are they able in geography?' This can alter the teachers' perspective of their pupils and may help to prevent real ability and talent from being overlooked or missed altogether. The list of suggestions given below shows how the approach to teaching about the Asian tsunami of 2004 might be varied and tasks set to cater for pupils' differing types of 'intelligence'.

Intelligence	Pupil may be able to . . .
Verbal/Linguistic	use reference books and other resources to write an essay or newspaper report on the impact of the hazard on the countries affected.
Logical/Mathematical	analyse data to show the frequency and magnitude of hazard events in the SE Asia region; construct graphs to quantify the impact.
Visual/Spatial	watch television reports of the tsunami; on a world map locate and mark on the areas affected with detailed annotations.
Bodily/Kinaesthetic	construct a model to show how the tsunami happened with reference to plate tectonics; simulate the effects of flooding.
Musical/Rhythmic	choose a piece of music to accompany images of the disaster and explain the choice.
Interpersonal	write a letter as someone involved in the rescue/emergency team to explain the effects of the tsunami on the lives of people in Indonesia.
Intrapersonal	write an account of the feelings of someone who lived through the disaster in the days and weeks after the event.

Multiple intelligences identification in geography – Asian tsunami 2004

Creativity and geography: Renzulli's three-ring model of giftedness

There is no one simple definition of what defines 'giftedness'. Joseph Renzulli (1977) proposed a three-ring model that incorporates not only ability in a particular subject but also elements of what he termed task commitment and creativity.

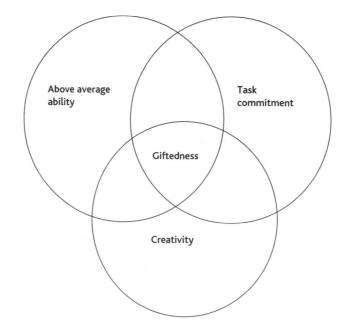

The model suggests that ability is not the sole determinant of giftedness and high achievement and, indeed, unless it is combined with other qualities, potential may go unfulfilled. Task commitment includes qualities such as motivation, determination, application, curiosity, enjoyment of and fascination with the subject, and resilience – in other words, not giving up when tackling more difficult concepts but working hard to attain the next level. The familiar phrase '1% inspiration, 99% perspiration' neatly sums this up. Creativity is also seen as important in Renzulli's model. Creativity could show itself in many ways but it is essentially the ability to think about or to approach ideas differently.

Case study – Leadership: Year 9 pupil showing exceptional performance

Kate's work is excellent in all respects and she complements innate ability with a keen desire to learn more. In group work she is a real leader, allocating roles, ensuring that all tasks are completed and helping others in appropriate ways. In a topic on Brazil, she came up with novel ideas such as the inclusion of music and she organised and led the presentation very maturely.

Some examples of how pupils might demonstrate giftedness by showing ability, task commitment and creativity are given below:

- pupils who take on a pedagogical role in the classroom, for example through presentations to the rest of the class, explaining viewpoints and answering or asking questions in discussion. This may help others to understand a new idea or issue as well as clarifying and deepening their own learning.

- pupils who think instinctively in a geographical way and have a high level of knowledge, understanding and skills, but who also think of different and alternative viewpoints, often going against expected ideas and opinions and veering into the controversial or offbeat.

- pupils who have the confidence and ingenuity to use analogies to help their own understanding, or to try to explain things to others.

- pupils who are able to look beyond the immediate and see interrelationships and the bigger picture.

- pupils who are able to synthesise their knowledge and understanding and draw links between different subjects. They understand complex ideas and can appreciate different viewpoints.

- pupils who challenge assumptions and show real independence of mind, arguing their particular viewpoint carefully but at the same time taking account of other peoples' ideas.

Case study – Different viewpoints, understanding complexity: Year 11 pupil (A*)

Hannah develops her ideas and understanding with excellent use of geographic terminology. She is able to appreciate the details and validity of two or more sides of an issue or argument and can also evaluate the relative importance of the different processes that lead to the formation of physical landforms.

Thinking skills and the able geographer

Developing higher order thinking skills is one way of challenging our more able geographers and, from the identification angle, pupils who are able to demonstrate these skills may well be those who have high potential. The five thinking skills outlined in the National Curriculum and running through the Leading in Learning strategy are: information-processing, reasoning, enquiry, creative thinking and evaluation. Some pupils may show all qualities, some just one or a few; but the ability to think in a higher order way, over and above the specific content of the work, is indicative of ability that should not be missed.

Case study – Beyond the classroom: Year 8 pupil working at Level 7

Melanie has a clear appreciation of the relevance of geography and a high level of spatial awareness. Her written and oral work is of a high quality and she has also been active on fieldwork, both actual and virtual, in public speaking, for example raising her concerns about a local bypass issue, and through taking part in the 'Worldwise' quiz and other geographical competitions.

If 'geography is everywhere', then all pupils have their own experiences of and thoughts about the world around them, whether locally or wider afield. Roberts (2003) refers to the 'personal geographies' of children, and those most able pupils may well be the ones who consciously or intuitively absorb experiences and can relate back to them in the classroom. So holidays and visits become important, especially if a teacher is able to capitalise on them. Nor should we forget that some highly able pupils do emerge from situations where there are fewer regular opportunities open to them; for example, there may be a lack of books at home, little access to a computer and only rarely visits or holidays. If these pupils demonstrate knowledge and understanding of a high order in spite of rather than because of circumstances, what more may it say about their innate ability and potential?

Case study – Walking encyclopedia: Year 7 pupil

Robert's CATs scores are not exceptional but his thirst for geographical knowledge is. He has a wide-ranging awareness of most aspects of the subject and acquires new information from reading widely and watching relevant television programmes. He is particularly strong on the scientific side, for example global climatic change, and writes at length, including details and data that many geography teachers may not know!

It is clear that there are a range of strategies which geography departments could use to identify the most able pupils and that using these strategies in combination is probably the best approach. Eyre (1997) makes the point that identifying high ability pupils is as much about sharing information as it is about talent spotting, since it is impossible to give a single definition of high ability. Using just one approach is likely to result in identifying the perennial high achievers, and not recognising specific ability in geography or those with potential to do well in the subject.

The importance of identification of the most able for schools and departments is so that they can provide effective and challenging opportunities which will stimulate and inspire these pupils to develop and allow them to reach their full potential. We cannot assume that the most able will do well simply because they are bright, they also need support, challenge, encouragement and opportunities. Identification is not an end in itself and is only valuable if it results in teachers changing and adapting their approach in the classroom to take account of their most able pupils.

Summary

- Pupils who are very able in geography are not necessarily identified by one checklist or set of criteria. Information from a variety of different sources should be used along with discussion about abilities and individual pupils.

- Identification of potential is also important. Able geographers may show their potential in a variety of ways.

- Departments need to monitor their lists of the more able at regular intervals to ensure that pupils are not being missed and that their potential is identified.

- How pupils learn most effectively, as well as what they learn, is important in terms of recognising ability and potential.

- Creativity and task commitment are both important components of giftedness or high ability.

- Identification of the most able is only worthwhile if it results in teachers adapting their practice to provide challenge and opportunities for these pupils.

CHAPTER 4

Classroom provision

- Recognising differences in preferred learning styles
- Geographical enquiry as a way to provide challenge
- Planning to support the most able in the classroom
- Differentiation
- Extension, enrichment and acceleration
- Developing skills needed by the most able
- Improving questioning technique
- Homework as a tool for stimulating the most able

The purpose of this chapter is to look at ways in which teachers can provide suitable challenge for their most able pupils within the geography classroom.

In his book *Lessons are for Learning*, Mike Hughes (1997) reminds us that pupils should 'leave a classroom at the end of a lesson knowing, understanding and being able to do more than when they came in'. It would be difficult for teachers to claim that this always happens, but it is perhaps the most able pupils who are most frequently short-changed, and all teachers, including geographers, have a responsibility to address this issue.

Many very able pupils are a pleasure to teach, but sometimes the most able are not easily motivated and do not appear to be curious or needing challenge. Indeed, some may be apathetic or lazy. Not all will use their abilities, and some can be uncooperative and unenthusiastic about class work and even disruptive. Teachers therefore need a range of strategies to encourage the most able to work to their full potential. This chapter will provide ideas that may be used or adapted by geography teachers to challenge the most able in the classroom. It is important to avoid providing the most able with lots of extra work, which may not be challenging. If possible, activities for the most able should be integrated and not simply bolted on in a way which neither extends nor stimulates their learning. In fact, if we are to really challenge our most able, we should expect them to be finding things difficult and to be getting some things wrong. Eyre (1997) argues that this is how 'the real learning takes place'.

Recognising differences in preferred learning styles

In recent years much has been written about learning styles and teachers have been encouraged to consider the learning preferences of their pupils. Although there is still much debate about the extent to which this is important, it is something which teachers should take into consideration, if only to add variety to their teaching. Some teachers feel both that they should take account of the preferred learning styles of their pupils in order to get the best out of them, and also that the pupils themselves should be aware of the ways in which they are likely to learn best. It is also important to help children develop the learning styles they may have less preference for. Some schools compile information about pupils' learning styles, but teachers can also find this out for themselves, either through observation or by using a short questionnaire such as the one in Appendix 4.1, which identifies learners as visual, auditory or kinaesthetic (VAK), a well understood approach to distinguishing preferred learning styles. However, all surveys such as this should be treated with caution.

The main characteristics of V, A and K learning styles

Visual (V) learners learn through seeing They prefer to read, to see words written down and to memorise by writing repeatedly. They may think in pictures and learn well from maps and diagrams, overhead transparencies, well illustrated textbooks and videos. These learners need to see the teacher's body language and facial expression to fully understand the content of a lesson and may prefer sitting at the front of the classroom to avoid visual obstructions. Visual learners often prefer to take detailed notes to absorb the information, and if they become bored they look around or doodle or watch something else.

Auditory (A) learners learn through listening They like to be told, to listen to the teacher and to talk about things. They often talk very fluently and in a logical order and memorise by repeating words out loud. They learn best through discussions, talking things through and listening to what others have to say, and written information may have little meaning until it is heard. These learners often benefit from reading text aloud and using a tape recorder.

Kinaesthetic (K) learners learn through moving, doing and touching They like to get involved and try things out and learn best through a hands-on approach. They may speak slowly and use lots of hand movements. They memorise by doing something repeatedly. They may find it hard to sit still for long periods and may become distracted by their need for activity.

It is also worth remembering that a teacher's own preferred learning style can dominate the way they teach in terms of their style, the resources they choose and the way they present information. Two useful books are *Accelerated*

Learning in the Classroom by Alastair Smith and *The Teacher's Toolkit* by Paul Ginnis.

All learners will use a combination of learning styles but many do have quite strong preferences for one learning style. Research by Specific Diagnostic Studies Inc. of Maryland USA reported in Ginnis (2002) suggests that, in general, 29% of people are mainly visual learners, 37% mainly kinaesthetic and 34% mainly auditory. Despite these statistics, much of what teachers present in the classroom depends wholly on pupils listening carefully to what is said. It is important to understand that pupils learn in different ways and therefore to use a variety of resources and teaching strategies to support this. However, it is also worth remembering that the most successful pupils are those who can access information in a variety of ways, so teachers should not allow pupils to work in their preferred learning style all the time but should encourage them to develop different learning styles so that they become more flexible and better all-round learners. The development of this ability is particularly important for the most able.

Geography is an ideal subject for providing a wide variety of learning experiences. Tabled below are examples of teaching resources and pupil activities appropriate to the different learning styles.

Learning styles	Teaching resources	Pupil activities
Visual	• diagrams • charts • well-illustrated text • photographs • pamphlets • the internet • OS maps • atlases • illustrated presentation	• spider diagrams • concept mapping • DARTs activities such as colour highlighting of text • web-based research • OS map work • annotating maps and diagrams • maps from memory
Auditory	• presentation • video with commentary • text which can be read out loud • radio broadcast • guest speaker • using music to introduce an issue	• discussion • group work or pair work • role play • interviews • storytelling • mind movies
Kinaesthetic	• presentation using the interactive whiteboard with pupil involvement • practical demonstrations	• model making • card sorting • concept mapping • fieldwork activities • games and simulations • role play • mysteries • living graphs • maps from memory • making animals

Tasks appropriate for different learning styles

DART strategies – Directed Activities Related to Text

Many classroom exercises, particularly comprehension exercises, allow pupils to pick through a text to find the 'right' answer without having to think very much or to understand what the text as a whole is about. In some cases, pupils may find text too difficult to understand because of its length, reading age or density. DART strategies, some of which are particularly appropriate for the most able, encourage pupils to think about what they are reading and to understand the meaning of the text. The strategies can also help pupils to access text that might otherwise be difficult for them to understand. For the most able, this approach can help them to handle dense and complex text, for example using articles found in the broadsheet newspapers, in magazines or on the internet.

DART strategies were devised by Lunzer and Gardner (1979). They encourage pupils to read and re-read text to understand the meaning. There are two types of DART strategies: reconstruction DARTs and analysis DARTs.

Reconstruction DARTs

Reconstruction DARTs involve pupils being given a modified version of the text; for example, the text is shortened or some words are deleted.

- **Diagram or table completion** Pupils are asked to read the text and use it to complete a table diagram, map or graph. It is useful for introducing geographical terms, for example features of headland erosion or plant succession in sand dunes, or for looking at land use in an urban area or at a hydrograph. Pupils are asked to read the text and use it to label the diagram, map, graph or table. This task can be differentiated by varying the amount of information left out of the diagram, but it can be quite demanding and thus suitable for the most able.

- **Sequencing DARTs** This is best used with text describing events which take place over a period of time, such as the eruption of a volcano or the development of a hurricane. The processes leading to the decline of an industrial area or the growth of a city would also be suitable subjects to use. Once suitable text has been found, the teacher needs to divide it into sections, then cut the text up into these sections and put them into separate envelopes for the pupils, who are then asked to arrange the text in the correct sequence. Including maps or diagrams which illustrate stages in the sequence also works well.

Analysis DARTs

In analysis DARTs, pupils work directly with the text as a whole and move on to present the ideas from the text in a different way, such as in a table or diagram.

- **Underlining or highlighting** Pupils are asked to underline particular ideas, such as arguments in favour of and against a plan, or the advantages and disadvantages of a scheme, and then to present their findings in another way, such as a table, or to write a report justifying their own viewpoint.

- **Text labelling** Pupils are given a text and asked to insert subheadings for paragraphs or sections. These subheadings are then used in another way, for example as the basis for some notes or to construct a table or diagram.

- **Constructing diagrams** Pupils can be asked to read text carefully and use it to construct a flow diagram or graph that presents the same information. This method can be used with processes such as global warming or eutrophication, or to describe how landforms develop.

Geographical enquiry as a way to provide challenge

Geography: The National Curriculum for England (DfEE 1999) emphasises the need for an enquiry approach to learning. The programme of study at each Key Stage starts with a paragraph that stresses the importance of enquiry (see below). Furthermore, enquiry skills are included in every level description in the Geography National Curriculum (GNC) attainment targets.

Enquiry skills in the Geography National Curriculum
Knowledge, skills and understanding

Teaching should ensure that geographical skills are used when developing knowledge and understanding of places, patterns and processes, environmental change and sustainable development.

Geographical enquiry and skills

In undertaking geographical enquiry, pupils should be taught to:

- ask geographical questions
- suggest appropriate sequences of investigation
- collect, record and present evidence
- analyse and evaluate evidence and draw and justify conclusions
- appreciate how people's values and attitudes, including their own, affect contemporary social, environmental, economic and political issues, and to clarify and develop their own values and attitudes about such issues
- communicate in ways appropriate to the task and to the audience

From *Geography: The National Curriculum for England*, programme of study for Key Stage 3, p. 22 (DfEE 1999)

The emphasis of both the programme of study and the attainment targets is on pupil involvement in the enquiry process. It is the pupils themselves who should 'ask geographical questions', 'suggest appropriate sequences of investigation' and so on.

In her book *Learning through Enquiry*, Roberts (2003) illustrates how geographical enquiry can occur in different ways, involving different degrees of participation.

	← ─── Closed ───	─── Framed ───	Negotiated →
Content	Focus of enquiry chosen by teacher.	Focus of enquiry chosen by students within theme (e.g. choosing which volcano to study).	Students choose focus of enquiry (e.g. choosing which less economically developed country to investigate).
Questions	Enquiry questions and sub questions chosen by teacher.	Teacher devises activities to encourage students to identify questions or sub questions.	Students devise questions and plan how to investigate them.
Making sense of data	Activities devised by teacher to achieve pre-determined objectives. Students follow instructions.	Students introduced to different techniques and conceptual frameworks and learn to use them selectively. Students may reach different conclusions.	Students search for sources of data and select relevant data from sources in and out of school. Students encouraged to be critical of data.
Summary	Teacher controls the construction of knowledge by making all decisions about data, activities and conclusions.	Teacher inducts students into the ways in which geographical knowledge is constructed. Students are made aware of choices and are encouraged to be critical.	Students are enabled, with teacher guidance, to investigate questions of interest to themselves and be able to evaluate their investigation critically.

The participation dimension in geographical enquiry (from Roberts, M. (2003) *Learning Through Enquiry: Making Sense of Geography in the Key Stage 3 Classroom*, the Geographical Association, p. 35)

Roberts emphasises that where the approach is 'negotiated', control is largely handed over to the pupil, with the teacher acting in a supporting role. The three categories shown in the diagram oversimplify the many different approaches that can occur within the classroom; however, the framework provides a useful point of reference when planning lessons aiming to provide challenge for the most able. Two important ways to develop enquiry skills, particularly with the most able, which should result in greater involvement, higher levels of thinking and a higher standard of work, are to:

- encourage pupils to start to negotiate and make decisions about their own learning, as this will mean they are likely to engage more thoroughly with their work and find lessons more stimulating and more enjoyable

- allow pupils more choice in, for example, the case studies used, and encourage them to collect their own information and evidence.

Overall, more able students respond very well to more open-ended tasks and to situations where they have some choice and flexibility in how to go about a piece of work. Indeed, in some cases, high achievement will only be shown when tasks are more open-ended and where there is more opportunity for choice. An example of how choice can be incorporated into a classroom activity is shown in the 'Pole to Pole' task in Appendix 4.2.

Planning to support the most able in the classroom

The geography curriculum needs to be planned at a number of levels: for the whole Key Stage, for each topic or unit, and for individual lessons. Most geography departments have schemes of work in place that outline key questions to be addressed, indicate the resources available and suggest the teaching strategies and types of assessment to be used. Detailed lesson plans, such as those insisted on during teacher training, are unlikely to be used on a daily basis by an experienced teacher (except perhaps to satisfy Ofsted). Nevertheless, clear planning, and preparation of resources, before all lessons is essential. Good teachers will also reflect on their lessons and evaluate strengths and weaknesses after each lesson and before teaching the same lesson again, with appropriate modifications. To cater adequately for the most able, teachers must consider their particular needs when writing schemes of work and when planning individual lessons.

As a first step, teachers should review schemes of work to consider whether the strategies being used are appropriate for challenging the most able, asking themselves such questions such as:

- Does the scheme of work incorporate enquiry-learning approaches?

- Are there opportunities for pupils to negotiate and make decisions about their own learning and/or to make their own choices, for example case studies?

- Does the scheme of work include a variety of approaches incorporating a range of learning styles?

- Are the assessment strategies varied and do they provide scope for the most able to demonstrate their ability?

Appendix 4.3 shows a four-week scheme of work from the Minster School in Southwell, Nottinghamshire, for Year 9 pupils studying a unit on development and globalisation. Learning outcomes are planned at three levels, showing that the most able are expected to develop more detailed knowledge and a deeper understanding of the issues, which will be evident in their assessment.

Individual lessons should be planned to incorporate ways to stretch the most able pupils. The following guidelines highlight what should be considered when planning schemes of work and individual lessons.

- **Set clear learning objectives** which take account of pupils' knowledge, understanding and skills. Recognise that the learning objectives for the most able may be different from the objectives for others in the class. The idea of 'all/most/some' seen in the learning objectives for the scheme of work in Appendix 4.3 can be introduced into individual lesson plans as 'must/should/could', to show the most able that they are expected to tackle some things which are not expected of everybody in the class. An example of this approach is provided in the 'Energy of the Future' task.

'Energy of the Future': an example of the 'must/could/should' approach

You have been asked to prepare a speech and argue the case for renewable energy at a conference called 'Energy of the Future'.

You must:

- Prepare the script for your speech. Explain to the audience the difference between renewable and non-renewable fuel. Give examples of each type. Convince the audience that they should use renewable fuels.

- Choose a suitable renewable fuel for use in Britain and another for use in Australia. Explain your choice for each.

You should:

- Prepare a hand-out to support your presentation. Describe in detail one method of generating electricity from a renewable source.

- Think about the arguments of those people who are not convinced about renewable energy and prepare answers to their points.

You could:

- Illustrate your hand-out with evidence such as statistics, charts and graphs that you can refer to in your presentation.

- **Use a variety of resources** and incorporate a range of learning styles in order to encourage pupils to become flexible learners.

- **Set a variety of tasks and activities** that provide different opportunities for pupils of different abilities. Avoid extension tasks that simply add 'more of the same'.

- **Provide opportunities to give plenty of feedback**, especially verbal feedback, and set clear targets for future learning.

When planning provision for the most able, it is important to think about which pupils will do the extension work. Deborah Eyre (1997) in her book *Able Children in Ordinary Schools* suggests a variety of methods to use when deciding who does extension work, according to the task being set. She suggests that sometimes the criterion could be speed, sometimes ability, sometimes choice, but points out that it is important to vary the way this is implemented to make sure the most able do not always have the opportunity to avoid extension work.

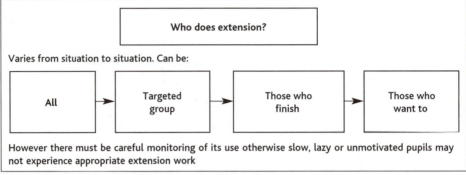

From Eyre, D. (1997) *Able Children in Ordinary Schools*, David Fulton Publishers, p. 42.

Differentiation

In February 2004 Ofsted reported that 'Teachers' expectations are lower (in geography) than in most other subjects'. One way to address this issue is for teachers to differentiate more effectively, particularly for their most able pupils. Differentiation needs to go beyond simply providing a task sheet which has extra questions for those who finish first, and teachers need to plan ways to intervene to help the most able to reach their potential. It is clear that simply adding 'more of the same' as an extension exercise at the end of a worksheet is not appropriate for challenging the most able. Indeed, these pupils will mostly need much less practice than other pupils to acquire skills or understand concepts: exercises which set yet more examples of, say, using six-figure grid references will not challenge those who were able to do it first time round. Yet another writing task bolted on to the end of the worksheet may not help the most able to learn more: these pupils do not want, or need, to be given more work simply to keep them quiet while others catch up.

The differentiation strategy diagrams opposite show a number of ways in which differentiation can be approached. These diagrams are a useful way of thinking about differentiation through varying the stimulus, the resources or the task. What the diagrams fail to emphasise, however, is that the amount of support the teacher provides and the expectations a teacher has of a pupil are also essential forms of differentiation. It is essential for teachers to encourage the most able to take on more challenging tasks and strive to complete these to a high standard.

Extension, enrichment and acceleration

The terms extension, enrichment and acceleration are often used to describe ways of providing suitable challenge for the most able. Extension material

Differentiation strategies

1. Differentiation by outcome: a common stimulus or resources such as a video, text or photograph is used, the task is the same for all pupils, for example some creative writing. Differentiation is by outcome with the most able being encouraged to produce more thorough work. This is a popular approach because it requires little extra preparation but it may not provide any degree of challenge for the most able, and it is easy for some to adopt a 'that will do' attitude to the work.

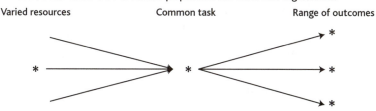

2. Differentiation by resources and by outcome: a range of resources targeted at specific pupils and taking their ability into account is provided. This enables more challenging resources to be provided for the most able; however, it also needs a lot of teacher preparation and classroom organisation.

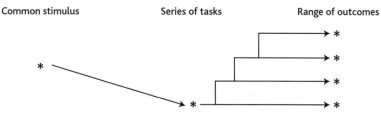

3. Differentiation by graded tasks and outcomes: all pupils use the same resources but follow a series of tasks or questions that may become increasingly demanding. The 'must', 'should' and 'could' approach can be used as part of this approach. It is also the way many exam questions are set.

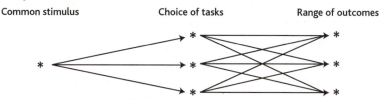

4. Differentiation by task and outcome: In this approach pupils have a choice of task as opposed to having extension exercises as in the example above. It means the most able can be given more difficult work from the outset and have to take some responsibility themselves for their learning. It is an excellent strategy but requires a lot of preparation in advance. Appendix 4.2 is an example of an activity differentiated by task and outcome.

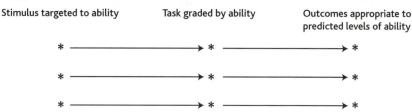

5. Differentiation by stimulus and task: teachers can provide different resources targeted at different abilities, for example three different pieces of text. It can be a useful technique for setting work for the most able but must be done on the basis of accurate knowledge of all pupils. It also requires a lot of advance preparation.

Stimulus targeted to ability	Task graded by ability	Outcomes appropriate to predicted levels of ability
* ⟶	* ⟶	*
* ⟶	* ⟶	*
* ⟶	* ⟶	*

Adapted from Lambert and Balderstone (2000) *Learning to Teach Geography in the Secondary School.*

usually adds depth; enrichment adds breadth; acceleration adds pace. All three can be useful approaches, either separately or in combination. However, none of them will be effective unless they provide challenge. Able pupils are rarely challenged by simply being given more practice of the same idea, or being asked to carry on to the next page of the book. Unplanned and unrewarded additional work or a very open activity is unlikely to stimulate the most able. Providing different resources, as in strategies 2 and 5 of the differentiation strategies detailed on page 57, or setting different tasks, as in strategies 3, 4 and 5, is usually a better approach than simply expecting more detailed and thorough answers or just adding extra work at the end of a common task, as in strategy 1.

Teachers should try to devise activities that challenge the most able to analyse, interpret and evaluate information and should encourage them to extend their thinking and encompass more complex ideas. Furthermore, it is important that the most able are encouraged to be active learners and not passive receivers of information. Challenging activities for the most able will include open-ended tasks and questions, clearly structured to allow the most able to forge ahead without having to repeatedly ask for instructions. Some possible approaches are the following.

Provide a task which allows choice and encourages research

The exercise entitled 'Pole to Pole' (Appendix 4.2) is an outstanding example of a task which really encourages more able pupils to produce work of a high standard. The unit of work can be introduced by looking at the first part of Michael Palin's Pole to Pole journey, which was shown on BBC TV in the 1990s and is now available on video. Pupils are then asked to imagine a journey starting at the North Pole, following a line of longitude and passing through at least five different countries, and to write a bit about each of these countries. The introductory video will engage the attention of all pupils and help them to become involved in the work that follows. Another reason why this approach is successful is that pupils have a considerable amount of choice within the task. They can choose which line of longitude they wish to follow and which countries they want to find out about. They can also choose how they record their findings – either as a diary entry, as an e-mail or postcard home, or on a tape – and they are encouraged to find pictures or other illustrative material where possible. This type of task is accessible to all pupils but provides opportunities for the most able to produce high quality work.

Provide scope for good quality extended writing

Much of the written work set by geography teachers is relatively undemanding, particularly where there is extensive use of closed questions. If pupils are asked, 'Explain what rural–urban migration is' or 'Describe how an ox-bow lake is formed', there is clearly a correct answer, even though, in providing it, some pupils may include more detail than others. Indeed, many GCSE and even AS level questions do not require more than three- or four-line answers, and many Key Stage 3 geography text books offer a double-page spread which includes short comprehension questions and little encouragement for extended writing. One of the main reasons for this is, undoubtedly, because it makes assessment easier. However, this should not be a reason to avoid extended writing tasks. The flexibility encompassed in the Geography National Curriculum allows scope for in-depth studies of some topics, if desired, which can be an ideal starting point for encouraging extended writing.

Two important reasons why writing skills should be developed are that:

- it helps pupils to learn to develop an argument, to structure their work, to analyse, to reason, to evaluate and to reach conclusions

- it helps teachers to find out more about their pupils and about how they are thinking and is a useful tool for formative assessment.

As Butt (2001) points out:

> We should not view all writing as an assessment 'end point': the mere culmination of what students know, understand and can do. Most writing is (or should be) a formative and educational activity.

It is important to provide pupils with a structure for any extended written work. One way of doing this is through card-sorting exercises, which provide background information and also encourage pupils to think about how to organise their ideas. In the example given in Appendix 4.4, pupils could sort the information into four categories: physical causes of cliff collapse, human causes of cliff collapse, the impacts of collapse, and possible management strategies. This would provide a framework for their written work, which could conclude with their own opinions about cliff protection in the area, and their justification for these opinions. If this exercise was done with a mixed ability group, a writing frame could be used to help the less able with the written task.

Encourage the use of more sophisticated geographical skills when analysing data

Census data for the local area can be obtained from www.neighbourhood. statistics.gov.uk. This can be used to plot data at ward level, using a base map showing wards and features such as the central business district (CBD) and industrial zones. Alternatively, the data could be used to produce graphs. The most able could be encouraged to produce choropleth maps or scatter diagrams instead of bar charts and pie charts. As an example, the 2001 census data for Sheffield wards, and some tasks using these data, are given on the website.

Providing data and asking the more able to select the best way to portray it and to justify their choice of method also provides more challenge than simply instructing them which method to use. Just as important would be to expect these able pupils to interpret their findings, exploring such questions as, for example, 'Is there any relationship between levels of unemployment and car ownership and, if so, why?' or 'Is it possible to identify areas of the city which experience deprivation and, if so, which parts of the city and why?'

Introduce problem-solving or decision-making exercises

Local issues often form a good basis for decision-making exercises. DART strategies (see earlier in this chapter) can help pupils to access text with a high reading age, for example, newspaper articles. For example, using different coloured pens to underline or highlight the arguments in favour of and the arguments against particular issues should enable pupils to summarise the main arguments and then to make and justify their own decision. Alternatively, they could be asked to identify the arguments of particular groups. Supplementary information, including maps and geographical background to the area, would enhance an exercise like this and emphasise the importance of place.

Use recent newspaper articles to stimulate and inform about global events

Teachers can access informative, up-to-date articles from the broadsheet newspapers either by cutting out articles or by downloading them from the newspaper websites. Websites of campaign groups or other non-government organisations (NGOs) are also a useful source of information. In articles such as this, it is interesting to try to distinguish between fact and opinion (see Leat 1998, *Thinking Through Geography*). Such an exercise encourages careful reading of the text but often leads to difficulties when pupils are unsure about how to decide if something is a fact or not. Thinking through how to overcome these difficulties can provide a good challenge for able pupils.

Encourage pupils to think about alternative futures

Curiosity, wondering about ideas, and imagining and thinking beyond the present are skills which should be encouraged in all pupils, including the most able. People's decisions and actions play a major part in events and can also change the course of future events. The future is shaped by decisions and actions taken from now onwards and, in order to achieve a better future, various 'alternative' routes should be considered. One approach is to pose an idea or a problem for pupils and ask how they would solve it; for example, ask them to think of an undesirable situation and consider how it could be changed to a more desirable one, such as 'overuse of resources', which is undesirable, and 'sustainable use of resources', which is desirable. Pupils should be encouraged to come up with a range of possible ideas for achieving this 'desirable' future, including ideas which seem unlikely or impossible.

Alternative futures (devised by James, aged 14)

The 'alternative futures' diagram shows some ideas put forward by a 14-year-old for solving traffic congestion in towns. A similar strategy could be used to ask pupils to think about alternative futures for the situations listed below.

Undesirable situation	Desirable situation
• Overuse of resources	• Sustainable use of resources
• Unemployment in . . . (or any area)	• Jobs for all in . . .
• Expanding shanty towns and poverty in LEDCs	• More good quality houses and less poverty
• Unfair trade	• Fair trade
• Rising sea levels and serious flooding resulting from global warming.	• Sea level rise and flooding managed effectively.

For each idea suggested, pupils should be encouraged to question how a better future could be achieved and what consequences it might have. Finally, the different routes could be evaluated in terms of impact on people and the environment, as well as in terms of how acceptable the plan might be politically. Adam Nichols developed this approach based on an idea from David Hicks (1994).

Use contrasting case studies to develop depth and breadth of knowledge

By encouraging more able pupils to look at case studies at a different scale or in a different part of the world from the example(s) used in class, you will help them to widen their knowledge. Giving pupils a choice about which areas they research and about the key questions they ask is likely to increase their engagement. The 'Pole to Pole' task in Appendix 4.2 provides an example of an exercise that has scope for pupils to make a number of choices. Internet-based research projects are another area where choice can easily be built into tasks.

Developing skills needed by the most able

It is important to encourage pupils to learn for themselves and to develop their capability to do so. It may be necessary to help the most able to develop the skills which will enable them to become more involved in their learning. This could require developing pupils' research skills, improving the way they explain their ideas, and encouraging them to think about how they think, their metacognition.

Research skills

With constantly improving access to the internet, the amount of resources available to pupils is enormous. Sophisticated search engines allow pupils to find out information quickly and easily, and many pupils have well developed research skills. However, there is a tendency to be over-reliant on the internet at the expense of other resources, and even the most able pupils may need help to filter through the available information, evaluate different resources and select what is relevant. Using a webquest such as the one shown in Appendix 4.5 is a useful approach.

- Encourage pupils to look for resources to supplement what they find on the internet, for example resources available in either the school library or the local reference library. Suggest the use of a variety of types of data in addition to text, for example maps, diagrams and data tables.

- Show pupils how to scan through their information and extract the relevant parts. Providing a framework such as a series of key questions or side headings will help them to decide what to retain and what to discard.

- Many pupils, even the most able, believe that everything they read in print is true. It is important to encourage them to evaluate the sources of their information. One way of doing this is to show how the same facts can be reported in very different ways by different organisations.

Explanation skills

Many pupils will give one-word answers to both oral and written questions, or else they will give very simplistic replies. For example, they will give the reasons for floods by simply saying, 'There was a lot of rain.' Or they will explain the decline of an industry by stating that it was affected by competition. Better oral and written explanations can be encouraged in the following ways.

- Encourage better oral explanations by using well-thought-out questioning techniques. It is important to probe and prompt pupils to develop their answers, and to give them enough time to think about their answer before providing it for them. One approach to developing oral explanations is to encourage pupils to become 'experts' in a particular field and then for them to share this information with others in the group. This is an activity in which the most able often thrive. One way of organising this is to challenge a small group, perhaps the most able, to become experts in a certain topic such as the sequence of events in the eruption of Mount St Helens, or the problems being caused by deforestation of the Amazon rainforest. This group is challenged to find out as much information as possible about this topic, using resources provided by the teacher or obtained from the library or the internet. The rest of the class meanwhile is asked to prepare a series of questions to ask the experts on their return.

- Encourage better written explanations by introducing a number of possible factors and asking them to discuss their relative importance. Using card-sorting activities that ask pupils to sort things into categories such as 'very important', 'quite important' and 'not important' would be one approach. A second way of encouraging pupils to think about how things are connected to each other is to ask pupils to construct a concept map based on a number of terms or ideas provided by the teacher. This is useful for the most able because it encourages them to look for interrelationships between factors, rather than for simple cause and effect. The figures which follow suggest some ideas that could be used to look at the causes of the Boscastle floods which occurred in August 2004.

About 70mm rain fell in two hours.	Cars parked in the car park were swept downstream.	Flash floods are not rare but they are difficult to forecast or prevent.
Two rivers meet in the village and water levels rose very rapidly.	Boscastle has many visitors in the summer.	Flood water 15 centimetres deep can sweep a person off their feet.
There had been a lot of rain in preceding weeks.	A field beside the river had been made into a car park.	Six buildings collapsed but many more were badly damaged.
The moorland above Boscastle was saturated.	Flash floods move at speed and are very forceful.	No one was killed, but several had to be airlifted to safety.
The bedrock in the area is impermeable granite.	The valley sides are very steep.	Global warming is causing a change in rainfall patterns.
There were reports of water 3 metres deep funnelling through the village.	Water and debris were trapped behind the bridges in the village.	Some of the oldest buildings in the village are built close to the river.

Concept mapping – the Boscastle floods, August 2004

Pupils should be given a large piece of paper, e.g. flip chart paper, and asked to write 'Boscastle floods' in the middle. They should then spread out the cards on the paper and draw arrows between any two where they can identify a link, and write on the arrow what the link is. For example, they could link 'There were reports of water 3 metres deep funnelling through the village' to 'Cars parked in the car park were swept downstream' and write 'Floodwater is strong enough to pick up cars' along the arrow linking the two. It should be possible to see many links between all the cards provided and it might also be possible to add other factors that could have been important. At this stage the teacher will need to prompt pupils to really explain the links. The next step would be to organise the ideas into a logical sequence before using them to write a full explanation of the causes and consequences of the Boscastle flood. A full discussion of using concept maps can be found in Nichols and Kinninment (2001) *More Thinking Through Geography.*

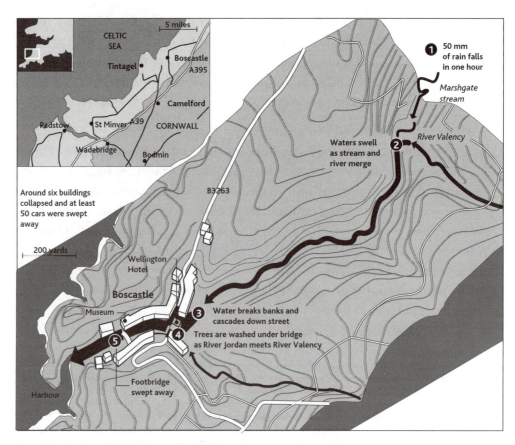

Map showing causes of Boscastle flood

Thinking skills or metacognition

A lot of attention has been drawn to the importance of teaching pupils to think, particularly by David Leat (in Fisher and Binns, 2000). Beyond this, however, it is also important for pupils to develop an understanding of how they are thinking. This 'thinking about thinking' is called metacognition. If teachers can help pupils to work out how they are thinking, then pupils may be able to apply the same approach to other problems or situations in the future. Leat's work with the Thinking Through Geography project (TTGP) is now well known (Leat 1998), and many of the strategies promoted by TTGP are particularly good for developing higher level thinking. For example: 'Mysteries, Fact or Opinion', 'Concept Mapping' and 'Layered Decision Making' strategies could all be used or adapted to provide appropriate challenge for the most able pupils. However, it is the debriefing that takes place during and after the activity which is particularly important for consolidating learning. Teachers need to challenge pupils to explain how and why they have made particular decisions and to share these ideas with the class. The teacher's role is crucial in questioning pupils and encouraging them to talk about their own thinking skills, to explain why they have made certain decisions, and to justify their answers. It is well worth looking at Kinninment and Leat's chapter 'Learn to debrief' in Fisher and Binns (2000) *Issues in Geography Teaching* to find out more about this approach.

Bloom's taxonomy

In 1956, Benjamin Bloom developed a classification of the levels of intellectual behaviour that are important in learning. Bloom identified six levels, from the simple recall of facts, as the lowest level, through increasingly more complex and abstract mental levels, to the highest level which he classified as evaluation. Examples of possible instructions which might be given to pupils are included at each level.

	Levels of thinking	Possible activities or tasks
Higher	Evaluation	evaluate, give an opinion, argue, assess, defend, decide, recommend, justify, conclude
	Synthesis	re-organise, arrange, propose, re-write, construct, plan, write a report, speculate, hypothesise
	Analysis	analyse, classify, order, explain, connect, compare/contrast, cause/effect, fact/opinion, criticise, correlate
	Application	apply, interpret, change or modify, relate
	Comprehension	describe, explain, locate, select, summarise, interpret, predict
Lower	Knowledge	list, define, underline, tell, describe, identify, show, label, collect, examine, tabulate, recall, remember, find information

Bloom's taxonomy – levels of thinking

These ideas are useful for teachers when deciding how to ask questions and what types of tasks to set on worksheets. The most able should be encouraged to apply their knowledge, to analyse findings, to synthesise and to evaluate. Using these levels of thinking as a guideline, it is possible to construct work that incorporates higher level thinking tasks for the most able.

Taxonomy of Swartz and Parks

Another taxonomy which is worth looking at is that produced by Swartz and Parks (1994). This is a non-hierarchical analysis of thinking skills that identifies different types of applications for thinking. Again, it is a useful starting point for teachers.

Improving questioning technique

Using questioning effectively is a good way for teachers to challenge more able pupils, but it is a teaching skill that needs practice. Wallace (2000) claims that 'the key to differentiation lies in the quality of teacher questioning.' There is considerable research evidence to show that teachers use questioning for class management and for recall of factual information but often fail to develop any form of extended questioning which would enable knowledge and understanding to be developed (Weeden *et al.* 2002). If a teacher's questioning skills are developed, then the most able children can be challenged and encouraged to clarify their ideas, to improve their explanations, to analyse, to evaluate and to justify their ideas. Skilful questioning can encourage pupils to think more deeply about issues being studied and to go away and find out more for themselves.

The work done by Paul Black, Dylan Wiliam and others on Assessment for Learning looks carefully at the role of questioning as a means of improving learning (Black *et al.* 2003). A starting point for their work on questioning was to discuss 'wait time', in other words the time allowed by teachers for a pupil to answer a question before the teacher moves on. Research in the USA by Rowe (in Black *et al.* 2003) found the average 'wait time' was less than one second, but Rowe also found that if the 'wait time' was increased, pupils gave longer answers, offered more alternative explanations and challenged or improved on the answers of others. Black and Wiliam (Black *et al.* 2003) encouraged teachers they worked with to increase wait times and, although many initially found this difficult, where they persevered they found it encouraged better, longer answers, more class discussion and more involvement with the lesson itself. They also looked at planning more carefully for questioning and at strategies to encourage discussion. The Key Stage 3 Strategy also adopted Assessment for Learning as a major initiative for schools from 2004 onwards, picking up on many of the ideas put forward by Black and Wiliam.

Some key points about questioning which might be particularly useful when considering how to challenge the most able are:

- Plan questions in advance as part of lesson preparation to make sure they are important in terms of pupil understanding.

- Try to ask open questions such as 'What do you think about the proposal to build a sea wall at . . .?' or 'Some people think that globalisation is a bad thing. Do you agree with them?' Closed questions (i.e. those which have a right answer, such as the meaning of geographical terms) are not useful as a way of providing challenge for pupils or as a way of encouraging higher order thinking.

- Ask probing questions which challenge and encourage pupils to explain, analyse, evaluate or solve a problem. For example: 'Why do so many people continue to live in San Francisco despite the likelihood that one day there will be a devastating earthquake there?' or 'How strong is the case for building new houses in the green belt in (location)?' or 'How can we measure traffic congestion in one area and compare it with that in another area?'

- Create a positive and trusting atmosphere in the classroom, so pupils will feel able to contribute. Encourage pupils to develop their answer and praise their attempts at doing so. Do not accept incorrect answers, but deal sensitively with wrong answers and correct any misunderstandings.

- Increase the 'wait time' after asking a pupil a question and before giving the answer yourself or moving on. Allow several seconds, do not intervene too quickly, and do not worry if there are periods of silence while pupils think.

- Encourage pupils not to put their hands up if they know an answer to a question. Pupils should be able to answer at any time, even if their answer is 'I don't know'. This 'no-hands-up' approach helps to keep all pupils focused and allows the teacher to ask the most able pupils more challenging questions.

- Try to promote discussion by asking pupils to think about other people's answers. For example, ask 'What could we add to Pat's answer?' or 'Can you see a connection between your answer and John's answer?'

- Use more advanced vocabulary and more complex language when asking questions to the most able and expect a more sophisticated response.

Questioning can be used in ways other than in a whole-class activity, and it is an important tool to use once the class are engaged in an activity. This provides the opportunity for more informal questioning, an ideal way to challenge the most able. By looking at work in progress, the teacher can provide immediate feedback and push the pupil to think more deeply or in a different way about an issue, asking such questions as: 'Why do you think that . . .?', 'How can you justify that . . .?', 'What is your opinion about . . .?' or, in a more speculative way, 'What if . . .?'

It is important to ask questions that challenge pupils to think, that require reasoning and encourage them to hypothesise. A useful checklist of possible questions is given below.

Questions to challenge the more able

Can you describe the distribution of...?

Can you give reasons for...?

Can you explain why...?

Could you put that in other words?

Why do you think that...?

Could you give some evidence to back that up?

Can you give me an example of...?

What sort of people would think that...?

Could you give me another point of view?

How could you argue against...?

What is your opinion about...?

Homework as a tool for stimulating the most able

Using differentiated homework is clearly a useful way to give the most able more demanding tasks or to introduce them to ideas that would not be accessible to others in the class. Homework can also be used to encourage independent work, especially where the class is working on an open-ended activity. More able pupils should be encouraged to use a range of resources to complete their homework, including books and other library resources and of course the internet. It is essential that teachers respond to homework that is set. This is an opportunity for teachers to communicate on an individual level with pupils, finding time to talk to them about their work, looking at what they have achieved, discussing problems or issues which they have found particularly interesting and setting them challenging targets.

Summary

- Teachers should provide suitable challenge for their most able pupils within the geography classroom.
- Teachers should review schemes of work with regard to learning styles, enquiry-led learning and opportunities for pupils to negotiate and make some of their own choices.
- Extension, enrichment and acceleration should be built into classroom activities.
- Challenging activities can be devised which help to develop skills in oral explanation, writing, data analysis, research and metacognition.
- Using questioning effectively can challenge more able pupils.

CHAPTER 5

Support for learning

- Underachieving able students
- Able students with special educational needs
- Case studies of gifted or talented pupils with special educational needs
- Making good use of school resources
- Revision strategies

Providing support for individuals and groups is an important aspect of working with the most able. At an individual level, teachers, teaching assistants, learning mentors, sixth formers or counsellors may offer this support, which may be social or emotional as well as academic.

All able pupils need support, but some groups need more support than others. These include underachievers and those with physical disabilities or other special educational needs (SEN). The geography book in the sister series 'Meeting SEN in the Curriculum' (Swift 2005) includes details of various special educational needs and the strategies that can be employed to help these students. Teachers should refer to that book for further guidance. However, the three conditions that are often associated with high ability – Asperger syndrome, dyslexia and attention deficit hyperactivity disorder (ADHD) – will be dealt with here.

Underachieving able students

Not all able pupils achieve highly, and teachers should try to identify able underachievers and try to support and encourage them to reach their potential. The primary purpose of support is to assist the learning process but, as Eyre (1979) points out, it may well be better to encourage more able students to struggle to resolve problems rather than to provide help at the first sign of difficulty 'because it is often at this point that the real learning occurs'. However, encouraging students to try to sort out difficulties for themselves should not be confused with neglecting them. Many able children describe with great indignation how they are left to drift or are given 'more of the same' while the teacher helps more demanding pupils. This neglect, as opposed to planned, delayed intervention, is one reason for the underachievement of some able children, but there are many other factors. It is important to realise that very able students need opportunities, support and encouragement in order to reach their full potential and make the most of their ability, and appropriate support is very important.

Why do able children underachieve?

Teachers need to ensure that they provide a learning environment which encourages all students, including the most able. Able children underachieve for a number of reasons. For example, they find the tasks they are given too easy, or too difficult, or simply lacking in purpose or relevance. Some find their teachers inflexible, overcritical or controlling, and some become stressed because of external exams. A common reason for underachievement is that students want to fit in with their peers and do not want to be seen as different or to be given extra work because of their ability.

It is not always easy to identify underachievers. Some students will actually try to hide their ability. Typical underachiever behaviour to look for includes giving up easily, or showing a marked difference between verbal ability and performance on written tasks (although this could also indicate specific learning problems). Some able students behave in an antisocial or attention-seeking way or try to blame poor performance on external factors, while others become withdrawn or show little self-confidence.

Case study – Peer group awareness

David is a very able boy. When in Year 9, he began to submit work of a very low level to fit in with his peers. His parents and teachers negotiated with him that he would give in other work to his teachers privately for which the teachers would provide written feedback that was not discussed in class, and that they would not give him end-of-term commendations as these drew attention to his true level of ability. After a year or so of this kind of support, David felt confident enough to be himself and to accept occasional comments from friends.

One group of students who have particular individual needs, but may also be particularly able, are children for whom English is not their main language. These may be children who have recently arrived in the country, but this group could also include students who use their own language at home and English at school. This can result in very able and articulate students who have difficulty in expressing their ideas in written English.

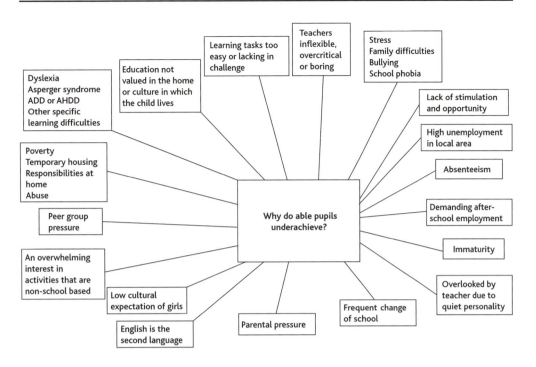

Where underachievement is general across most subjects, teachers will need to support students by:

- working with experts within the school (learning mentors, teaching assistants, the SEN coordinator) and possibly also with parents to identify reasons for underachievement. A school-wide and departmental plan to address the problems will need to be developed

- being sensitive to any difficulties the student is experiencing

- setting realistic targets to break the cycle of underachievement. Able children often underestimate their abilities and may need many small steps to achieve what they are capable of rather than huge steps that outface them

- working through students' strengths or interests.

Where students are underachieving only in geography or one or two subjects, teachers will need to look carefully at their teaching, at the subject matter, at the content of individual lessons and at how the content is being delivered. It is worth asking questions such as:

- Are students stimulated by what they are learning, can they see its relevance and are they curious to know more?

- Are lessons varied and engaging and taught in a way that generates enthusiasm?

- Are the approaches and tasks sufficiently challenging or even too challenging?

- Are the approaches and tasks varied enough to enable all students to have some opportunity to work through their preferred learning styles? Is there a balance of visual, auditory and kinaesthetic activities?

- Are specific skills required with which the student has difficulties? – e.g. map reading, careful measurement, orientation

- Is there something in the classroom environment that makes it difficult to concentrate or participate?

- Are enough structured comments being given to the students, in language they can understand, so that they know exactly what they need to do to achieve more highly?

- Are pupils being involved in setting their own targets or in formative assessment such as peer and self assessment?

- Are students' particular strengths being built on?

Case study – Developing specific skills

Jack is in Year 8 and finds it difficult to develop relationships with adults, including teachers. He is articulate and has excellent ICT skills, but he will avoid having to write anything down if possible. In geography, his strengths are encouraged and his teacher has been able to get him to act as a leader when reporting back from group work. Jack is also a good mentor helping others with ICT activities, and he has worked with a small group to research designated websites. This strategy of developing Jack's strengths and building on his own success is helping him to understand that, at times, written work is important. This has led to an improved attitude towards his work.

Able students with special educational needs

Although this chapter mainly looks at ways of supporting all very able children, it is important to recognise that gifted children with special educational needs exist. These could include students with the full range of physical disabilities, dyslexia, attention deficit disorder with (ADHD) or without (ADD) hyperactivity, and Asperger syndrome. Montgomery (2003) uses the term 'double exceptionality' to describe students such as these and points out that 'from the intervention point of view, the most obvious sign of difficulty is the special need; the other, the giftedness, is regarded as a bonus.'

It is important for teachers to be aware that despite their special needs these students may be capable of achieving very highly. The teacher may need to expect the unexpected – for example, a child with Asperger syndrome who can name all the capital cities in the world. It is important to develop strategies to encourage and provide challenge for these pupils. The table opposite shows the three special needs which are most likely to be experienced in combination with high intellectual ability – dyslexia, ADD or ADHD, and Asperger syndrome – together with some possible strategies for teachers.

	Typical characteristic	Useful strategies for the geography classroom
Dyslexia This is a neurological disorder that can significantly affect a person's ability to cope with words. There are a range of symptoms including difficulties with reading, writing, spelling and organisation. Dyslexia can occur at any level of intellectual ability.	• Reading requires effort and concentration. Pupils may frequently lose their place while reading, make a lot of errors with the high frequency words, have difficulty reading names and have difficulty blending sounds and segmenting words. • Work may seem messy with crossings outs, similarly shaped letters may be confused, such as b/d/p/q, m/w, n/u, and letters in words may be jumbled: tired/tried. Spelling difficulties often persist into adult life and they may become reluctant writers.	• Provide structure for written work and encourage the use of word processors, or spell checkers. • Consider recording information as mind maps, pictures, flow diagrams or using audio recording methods. • Provide photocopies of work written on the board and key word lists. • Encourage them to be responsible for reporting back in group work. • Allow extra time for tasks including assessments and exams.
Attention Deficit Disorder (with or without hyperactivity) ADD or ADHD This term is used to describe pupils who exhibit overactive behaviour and impulsiveness and who have difficulty in paying attention. It is genetic and caused by a form of brain dysfunction. ADD and ADHD can occur in pupils of all levels of ability.	• Pupils have difficulty in following instructions and completing tasks and can be easily distracted by noise or movement of others. • Pupils may not listen when spoken to. They may fidget and become restless and may interfere with other students' work by constantly talking, calling out or interrupting others. They often have difficulty in waiting or taking turns. • Pupils act impulsively without thinking about the consequences.	• Sit the pupil away from obvious distractions such as windows or the computer. • Use the pupil's name whenever possible, make eye contact when speaking. • Make instructions simple and tell the pupil when to begin the task. • Give advance warning when something is about to change e.g. 'In two minutes I need you (pupil name) to . . .' • Give specific praise for effort, achievement and positive behaviour. • Give the pupil responsibilities to help others, for example encouraging them to report back from group work. • Ask for specific advice from the SEN department when these pupils are involved in fieldwork.
Asperger syndrome This is a disorder at the able end of the autistic spectrum and people with this syndrome can have high intelligence. They have impaired motor skills often finding difficulty in writing. Boys are more likely to be affected than girls.	• An inability to understand the complex rules of social interactions means pupils find it difficult to make friends. Social situations such as lessons can cause great anxiety. • Pupils often excel at learning facts and figures but have difficulty understanding abstract concepts. They often have an all-consuming special interest. • Pupils may sound rather pedantic when speaking, often with little expression. They have difficulty understanding non-verbal language such as facial expressions and eye contact. They have a literal understanding of language, and do not grasp implied meaning.	• Create a calm classroom environment and allow the pupil to sit in the same place each lesson. • Give pupils time to think about questions and wait for their response. • Make sure the pupil understands what to do and give written instructions particularly homework, which should be stuck into the exercise book or planner. • Give advance warning when something is about to change e.g. 'In two minutes I need you (pupil name) to . . .' • Avoid group work, these pupils often work better in pairs. • Always apply rules consistently. • Ask for specific advice from the SEN department when these pupils are involved in fieldwork.

Working with able pupils with special educational needs in geography

Case studies of gifted or talented pupils with SEN

Michael – dyslexic (Year 9)

Michael obtained a place at a boys' grammar school but has struggled ever since. He has an extensive vocabulary and always volunteers for drama productions and reporting back when working in a group. He enjoys music, art and design technology (DT) and brings a keen imagination and wit to all these subjects. Michael prefers the company of teachers and older pupils, with whom he likes to debate topical issues. His peers, on the other hand, regard him as a 'bit of a wimp' as he does not enjoy sport and frequently corrects their behaviour.

After a very slow start in early childhood, Michael can now read fluently but his other problems associated with dyslexia remain. His spelling and handwriting are very poor. He finds it almost impossible to obtain information from large swathes of text. Even when the main ideas are summarised for him in bullet points, he still has difficulty revising for examinations or tests or picking out and organising the main ideas for an essay. In maths, he is criticised for the chaotic layout of his work but he finds it difficult to organise things in a way that is logical to other people. His family are very supportive and give him a lot of help with homework, so much so that teachers are sometimes misled into believing that he is coping well, until his difficulties are highlighted by his very poor performance in written exams.

Because he is so articulate, Michael is able to explain his frustrations to his teachers who are, on the whole, sympathetic. However, they are not very helpful in providing him with useful strategies.

Strategies

- Liaise with the SEN team so that your approach with Michael fits in with their overall support programme for the boy.

- Teach Michael to mind map so that he can use this skill to record information and revise if he finds this helpful.

- Encourage Michael to remember facts by making audio recordings or setting them to music.

- Make sure that Michael's homework tasks are suitable for his level of ability but are modified to allow him to succeed. For example, give him a template of notes with key words missing rather than asking him to make his own notes.

- Encourage Michael to wordprocess some homework and insist on careful use of a spellchecker.

- Use field trips and group activities to highlight and develop Michael's artistic, imaginative and reporting-back strengths.

Trevor – ADHD (Year 8)

Trevor had a very high aggregated CATs score when he entered his comprehensive school but was described by his primary teachers as having a 'self-destruct button'. He is a bundle of contradictions. On good days he is capable of being charming and polite. Sometimes he becomes so engrossed in an activity that it is hard to draw him away from it. He loves books, especially those with detailed maps and diagrams in, and likes to share what he has found out with teachers and other adults. He is a natural actor and sings and looks like an angel.

Yet Trevor is equally capable of destroying a lesson with his extremely disruptive and increasingly dangerous behaviour. He will erupt from his chair and turn on a machine just as someone puts their hands near it. His science teachers have had to give up all practical lessons and lock the preparation room when he is around because he uses his intelligence and wide reading to destructive effect. He has an intense dislike of writing and rarely does class work or submits homework. In mental arithmetic he excels, although he is reluctant to allow classmates many opportunities to show what they know.

For a small band of troublesome peers, he is a hero. Most other pupils laugh at his antics but find him very disturbing. They are rarely brave enough to offer criticism.

His mother will not acknowledge that there is a problem and refuses to consider medication or psychiatric help.

Strategies

- Investigate the possibility that Trevor is also dyslexic if this has not already been done.

- Agree a school-wide policy of support, and even containment, for Trevor.

- Prioritise what behaviour or work is to be achieved by Trevor and put in place a reward system. It might be best to make no demands as far as written work is concerned until the behaviour has been dealt with.

- Invite Trevor's mother to sit in on some lessons where the problems are most severe and keep trying to work with her.

- Make a careful risk assessment before taking Trevor off-premises, and make sure that a teaching assistant, learning mentor or similar is supervising him the whole time.

Malcolm – Asperger syndrome (Year 7)

In spite of careful liaison between the primary school and the head of Year 7, teachers were still taken by surprise when they met Malcolm. They had not appreciated that he would have to be taught many things that other children pick up by observation. For instance, he did not understand about queuing for his lunch and simply crawled between everyone's legs to get to the food.

His speech is robotic, and it can be disconcerting when he does not give the expected answer but simply says whatever is in his head at the time. He does not understand tact and might say, 'That dress is old', without appreciating that this could give offence. Sometimes he becomes obsessed by a door or window and wants it opened to a particular angle. This same obsession is apparent in his written work, where he can become anxious if teachers try to persuade him to set it out in a different way.

He is a very able mathematician and should reach university level in three or four years. However, he cannot cope with group work or group investigations and will become quite agitated if put into such a situation. Malcolm is also an outstanding chess player and was representing the school within a few weeks of arriving. In all other academic subjects he copes quite well in the top set, although his very literal understanding of some concepts can create problems, particularly in English.

Sport is a mystery to him. He does not understand the rules and is, in any case, lumbering and ungainly. It is during these lessons that his peers are most likely to be unkind, although, on the whole, they are quite protective towards him.

Strategies

- Find out how Malcolm's condition has been explained to him by his family and make sure that all teachers in the department are aware of this.

- There should be coordinated support for Malcolm across the school. One person should be responsible at school and department levels for monitoring him on a regular basis and dealing with any recurrent problems.

- Teach Malcolm any social skills he lacks in a very simple, direct and non-judgmental way. For example: 'When someone says, "How are you?", you say, "Fine, thank you".'

- Where Malcolm finds group work distressing, he could work as part of a pair when he has a specific task to accomplish that does not demand long periods of interaction.

- When large group work is required, give Malcolm a task that is important to the success of the group but can mostly be completed by him on his own.

- Encourage other pupils to be proud of Malcolm's achievements for the school when he plays in the chess team.

- Before any field trips, explain carefully to Malcolm what is going to happen and how he should behave when certain things occur. Make sure that someone who knows him well and is alert to signs of distress and confusion supervises him. Find out from parents/carers in advance if there are 'triggers' that might provoke disturbed behaviour.

Making good use of school resources

Schools and departments that are successful in stimulating their most able students make good use of their resources, whether human or otherwise. It is important to have flexibility and to adopt a creative approach to providing and accessing resources and support for the most able pupils.

Learning mentors, teaching assistants and others

Some schools help the most able by assigning teaching assistants and learning mentors the task of supporting them. Some assistants and mentors receive a general training either on-site or elsewhere, and others are trained as counsellors. Excellence in Cities areas pioneered this approach and other areas are following suit. Sixth form students can also be used to support more able pupils and of course many parents or carers are also happy to be involved. Some children may be resistant to help from home, and indeed parents themselves may be reluctant to get involved for fear of 'doing the wrong thing', so a direct approach to parents or carers may be helpful.

Learning mentors can:

- help in setting academic and other targets

- monitor progress and alert staff where students feel anxious, bored or pressured

- befriend able children who are isolated

- deal with behaviour problems

- act as a go-between where able students have conflicting commitments both within and beyond school.

Teaching assistants can:

- work on extension tasks with groups of students

- supervise other pupils while the geography teacher works with the most able

- provide feedback and show an interest in what able students have achieved while the geography teacher is working with others

- work with small groups of able students on research tasks in the library or resource centre or supervise them off-site.

Case study – Internal mentoring programme

A mentoring programme was set up for Year 8 pupils at All Saints Catholic School, Dagenham, to monitor progress of the gifted and talented cohort. The aim was to provide support for the most able by reviewing their progress and setting targets and to look at the value of activities offered through the G&T programme.

A team of staff was identified to take on the mentoring role. They were given information about the pupils including SATs and CATs, enabling them to build up profiles. The programme started in September 2002 and mentors were allocated one 50-minute period a week for mentoring, usually allowing them to talk to two students each week. A key aspect of the session was target-setting, and mentors drew on work which students were doing in class and used a simple form to record progress, student views or issues, targets and action needed.

Before the project started there was no support for more able pupils; this programme led to better understanding of their needs and greater awareness of the impact of the G&T programme. Senior management were supportive and staff reaction to the project was positive. The sessions helped to identify and respond to individual needs of students, who valued the opportunity to talk about their needs with mentors. The mentoring project was also valuable in helping to identify early entrants for GCSE and in generating more support for the G&T coordinator.

(From DfES Standards website case studies. Author Janet Dyson. www.standards. dfes.gov.uk/giftedandtalented/goodpractice/cs)

Case study – Employment of an outside counsellor

A school in Lincolnshire decided to focus attention on able underachievers. A counsellor was employed to interview these students in order to pinpoint factors contributing to their underachievement. She produced notes on the learning styles of the pupils and the aspects of school life that frustrated them, including extracurricular activities that were not available. Pupils talked enthusiastically about their relationship with this counsellor and how much they appreciated having a non-teacher to confide in. They were also encouraged by the recognition of their abilities. Teachers also found it helpful to learn which subjects/topics were disliked and why. The exercise was considered so valuable that this counsellor is now being funded out of beacon money.

(From *Schools Facing Challenging Circumstances* DfES Report 2004)

Sixth formers and other senior pupils can:

- act as mentors either with able individuals or small groups of able students

- act as befrienders where younger students are isolated or subject to bullying

- be used to extend/challenge able students who need more attention than the teacher can provide

- help with revision programmes

- help with extracurricular activities, e.g. an environmental club or a group involved with campaigns such as Fair Trade

- help with revision.

Parents and carers can:

- encourage their children to watch TV programmes about geographical issues

- involve children in planning visits and holidays, and encourage them to use maps and atlases

- discuss local or global events which are reported in the news, e.g. natural hazards, attitudes to climate change and issues about trade and aid

- discuss homework topics and encourage their children to look for a range of resources using books and the internet.

Libraries and resource centres

The content of many school libraries and resource centres is often unbalanced, reflecting the interests and knowledge of the librarian or the activity of a particular teacher or department. Libraries are not always well used because there is not enough dialogue between teachers and librarians and because students do not know how to use reference systems and search engines.

On the other hand, the library is a wonderful resource and, by working with the librarian or learning resource manager, geography teachers should be able to help students to access a wide range of resources.

Geography teachers should:

- provide librarians/resource managers with lists of books and other resources that should be available in the library for geography

- set up activities which can take place in the library, preferably during lesson time, and include the librarian/resource manager in their planning. The 'Pole to Pole' activity described in Appendix 4.2 is an example of an enquiry that is best done in a library or resource centre

- alert librarians/resource managers to topics that students might be researching and provide them with lists of websites/books/CDs/tapes that students might use. The 'Energy for the Future' exercise in Chapter 4 is an example

- make sure that librarians/resource managers are aware of who the most able students are, and what resources they should be directed to

- ask librarians/resource managers to look out for resources for particular aspects of the geography curriculum

- alert librarians/resource managers to able pupils with SEN who may need help accessing particular resources

- press for pupils to receive training on the evaluation of materials found on the internet. Even very able students do not always recognise that a source is unreliable or biased.

Librarians and resource centre staff should be involved in all school INSET concerning more able students.

Departmental resources

- Build up a departmental library containing a range of resources including books, geographical magazines, material from NGOs such as Oxfam or Friends of the Earth, videos, DVDs, CDs and newspaper cuttings.

- If there is only one geography teaching room equipped with computers, TV and video/DVD player or digital projector, then make sure all geography teachers and their classes have regular access and that use of this room is rotated between staff and classes.

- Look through all departmental resources regularly and remove old or outdated items such as old atlases, outdated text books, or newspaper articles which are several years old.

- Provide all geography teachers with a list of resources available within the department and their suitability for different groups. It is important to update this list regularly as resources change. This list of resources may well form part of a departmental handbook.

Revision strategies

Teachers are increasingly aware of the need to provide good quality help with revision for all pupils taking examinations. The most able can benefit as much as anyone from this input, whether it be specifically targeted revision classes, use of commercially produced revision guides or online help.

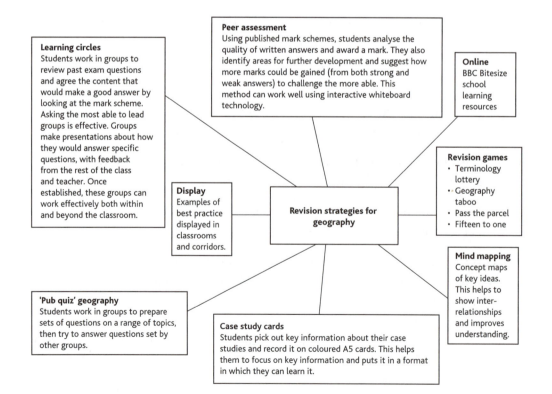

Learning circles
Students work in groups to review past exam questions and agree the content that would make a good answer by looking at the mark scheme. Asking the most able to lead groups is effective. Groups make presentations about how they would answer specific questions, with feedback from the rest of the class and teacher. Once established, these groups can work effectively both within and beyond the classroom.

Peer assessment
Using published mark schemes, students analyse the quality of written answers and award a mark. They also identify areas for further development and suggest how more marks could be gained (from both strong and weak answers) to challenge the more able. This method can work well using interactive whiteboard technology.

Online
BBC Bitesize school learning resources

Display
Examples of best practice displayed in classrooms and corridors.

Revision strategies for geography

Revision games
- Terminology lottery
- Geography taboo
- Pass the parcel
- Fifteen to one

Mind mapping
Concept maps of key ideas. This helps to show inter-relationships and improves understanding.

'Pub quiz' geography
Students work in groups to prepare sets of questions on a range of topics, then try to answer questions set by other groups.

Case study cards
Students pick out key information about their case studies and record it on coloured A5 cards. This helps them to focus on key information and puts it in a format in which they can learn it.

Summary

- Some groups of able children need more support than others.

- Able children may underachieve for a number of reasons. Teachers should be aware of this group of able children and try to address their needs.

- A small number of able children also have special educational needs. Teachers need to understand their particular difficulties and develop strategies to help.

- Using other adults to help support the most able can be helpful, e.g. learning mentors, teaching assistants, sixth formers and parents or carers.

- It is important to make full use of school resources, including libraries and resource centres, and to develop departmental resources where possible.

- Able children can benefit from targeted revision sessions.

CHAPTER 6

Beyond the classroom

- Fieldwork visits
- Competitions and other projects
- Enrichment and extension activities
- Challenge days and masterclasses
- Summer schools
- Links with universities
- Links with business and other organisations

The purpose of this chapter is to look at how activities outside the classroom, including fieldwork and links with organisations such as universities and businesses, can stimulate interest and provide challenge for the most able, as well as enhancing learning for all pupils. Away from the classroom it is often easier for teachers to focus on the needs of the more able, either as part of what the whole class is doing, or by developing specific activities for the more able and allowing them to work in pairs or in a small group. It is worth looking again at the 'Who does extension?' diagram in Chapter 4, which suggests different ways in which teachers might select pupils to do extension work, for example by choosing a targeted group, or by choosing those who finish tasks early, or simply by giving extension work to those pupils who wish to do it.

Organising extracurricular activities for a selected group of gifted pupils has some particular advantages. First, the activity can focus entirely on the most able and can be designed to include pupils from different year groups. The activities themselves can be more challenging and demanding if they are aimed only at the most able, and the students will benefit from each other's ideas. In such a situation, some students may feel less inhibited and so ask more questions or put forward more ideas. Focusing on a relatively small number of students means it may be possible to transport them all by minibus or even by public transport. Also, it may be easier to involve other educational organisations or local businesses with a small group. An obvious disadvantage of such targeted activities is the cost involved in terms of time and money. A school may be unwilling to release staff for a day or more, and there may be difficulties in securing funding for transport or accommodation. Schools may have a G&T budget but, otherwise, teachers need to be proactive in terms of negotiating funding with their head teacher or obtaining it from other sources. Geography-led schemes often have links to other areas of the curriculum or can be seen to be of value as a whole-school initiative and it is worth considering these aspects when arguing for support for a particular project.

Fieldwork visits

Few geography teachers need to be convinced of the value of field visits as, despite the increasing bureaucracy involved in organising them, they are invaluable experiences for both staff and pupils. Butt (2000) points out:

> Fieldwork activities should be engaging and motivational, often involving group work and self direction.

And it is this aspect that makes fieldwork an ideal way to involve and challenge the most able. It is beyond question that fieldwork can help to stimulate a genuine interest in the subject and the experience of geography in the field may inspire a long-term enthusiasm for the subject. Field visits can encourage pupils to pursue geography for GCSE or A level or even to choose to study geography at university. Some useful ways of thinking about different approaches to fieldwork are shown on the following page.

Visiting established educational centres can provide excellent inspirational opportunities for geographers. Examples of centres to visit are the Earth Galleries at the Science Museum in London, Urbis in Manchester and Our Dynamic Earth in Edinburgh, and there are many more. Some centres have free entry; others charge, but schools will usually be able to negotiate a favourable rate. Some offer organised visits and some provide worksheets for teachers to supervise; however, teachers may prefer to devise their own activities and tailor them to the needs and interests of the particular group. These visits are likely to be teacher-led and fall into Job's 'earth education' or 'field excursion' categories (see following page).

'Enquiry fieldwork', 'hypothesis testing' and 'discovery fieldwork' are more likely to take place during visits to sites such as a local river or coastline, an area of urban redevelopment, or a rural or urban area contrasting with your own. A site visit by the teacher in advance of the group visit is essential, and with successive visits the teacher will have the confidence to develop and modify the field visit programme.

Field visits may take place within the school day, but if the visit duration can be extended into the evening, over a weekend or even longer, there can be lots of benefits. Many teachers are happy to organise their own visits but there are also a number of organisations, such as the Field Studies Council, which run day and residential fieldwork courses which can be tailored to your own requirements. Some schools are able to organise visits to European destinations including

Some Types of Fieldwork

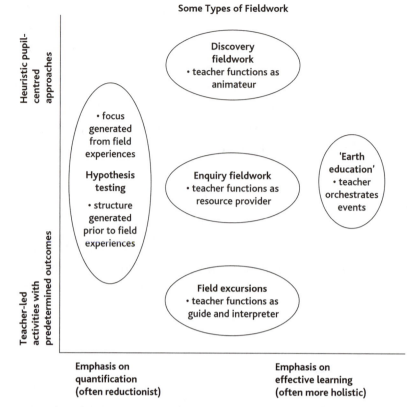

Taken from Job, D. (1996) 'Geography and environmental education – an exploration of perspectives and strategies' in Kent, A., Lambert, D., Naish, M. and Slater, F. (eds) *Geography in Education: Viewpoints on Teaching and Learning*. Cambridge University Press.

Iceland, or further afield to the USA or even to parts of Africa or South East Asia. These visits are particularly good for older students, perhaps those aspiring to A level; they provide a wider view of geography and an opportunity to look at issues in a different context. There are companies which organise visits like this and it is well worth being bold and adventurous if you can be. However, for many schools, field visits to other parts of Britain – or even within the school's own local area – are a more realistic option. Such field trips can prove extremely useful experiences for all students, including – with appropriate planning – the most able.

Fieldwork provision for the more able

The following examples show ways in which provision for more able pupils can be achieved on field visits.

Fieldwork for all, with discrete activities organised for the most able

As part of their GCSE coursework, the Minster School in Southwell, Nottinghamshire, organises a fieldwork visit to a river in an upland area to investigate river flow characteristics. The group of 45 pupils investigate river velocity by using floats and stopwatches to collect average speed data. More able pupils are shown how to use flow meters, which allows them to collect additional data across the river at systematic intervals and at varying depths.

This then allows surface speed to be compared with average velocity at depth, particularly at meanders, which are a core aspect of the study. The data can be used to construct isoline diagrams showing river velocity, and pupils are asked to compare data between the inner and outer bends of the meander and to suggest reasons for the differences. Thus the coursework tasks can be differentiated, providing more challenge for the most able pupils.

Fieldwork organised specifically for a group of very able geographers

King Edward VII School in Sheffield has organised a day's fieldwork towards the end of the autumn term specifically for their most able Year 11 students. Up to 14 pupils, 10–15% of a typical Year 11 geography cohort of about 100, are selected for their ability and enthusiasm in geography. The pupils are taken to a youth hostel in the Peak District, where a study room and meals can be booked on a daily basis. Various activities have been developed over the years, including a river study comparing characteristics of streams of different orders, rural settlement studies and evaluating flood management strategies. After an introduction to National Park issues which takes place at the youth hostel, the group go into the field to collect data, returning by mid-afternoon as it gets dark. Sophisticated data analysis techniques are introduced to challenge the students, such as bed load analysis, or the use of a centrality index to compare rural settlements. After an evening meal in the youth hostel, the day concludes with a role play, or with pupils making group presentations about their findings. This format encourages challenge in a less formal atmosphere than the classroom and often helps to develop a real enthusiasm for geography amongst the participants.

Residential fieldwork on a cross-curriculum basis

In 2004, three secondary schools in Sheffield – Firth Park, Wisewood and King Edward VII – organised a joint venture for gifted and talented Year 9 pupils. Residential visits have been organised by this cluster of schools over a number of years, and in 2004 the focus was geography, French and history. Pupils were selected for a place on the basis of their completing a detailed A3 geographical fact file on France, written in both English and French. The visit was designed to extend the learning experiences and provide challenge for the pupils in ways which would be difficult in a classroom setting. The cross-curricular experience included visits to the Normandy beaches and Rouen, as well as looking at settlement structures and at coastal geomorphology at Étretat. Visits such as this need funding and support from schools but can clearly provide huge benefits in many ways. It is worth investigating contacts other departments might have, such as exchange visits organised by the languages department, and developing ways of working together.

Fieldwork in a less economically developed country (LEDC)

Field trips abroad will not be for all schools and departments, and they need not necessarily be geography-led. If they are undertaken, however, from the very first stepping out of the coach or plane, there will be a great many opportunities for widening both the eyes and the minds of pupils. In an unfamiliar and very different setting, more able geographers are capable of displaying naturally enquiring minds as they take in a wealth of information, often relating to ideas and issues previously discussed in the classroom. A field trip in an LEDC is stimulating geography in itself, and there are often opportunities to push the thinking of the more able and challenge them further. In Kenya, based at the Marich Pass field study centre in the Rift Valley, an exercise called 'The Pokot: portrait of a subsistence economy' was carried out by a school group. This exercise led to discussions about local tribespeople and the understanding of concepts such as appropriate technology and the value of aid and development schemes. It is also valuable for pupils to consider the significance of their own presence as visitors to a particular location, on a field trip or as tourists, as a focus for geographical discussion.

Planning fieldwork activities

As is the case with classroom activities, simply arranging fieldwork visits does not automatically provide challenge for the most able. What is important are the activities planned and how involved the pupils are in making decisions. When fieldwork activities for the most able are being designed, tasks involving more complex geographical ideas and skills must be incorporated. It is an ideal situation to use enquiry-based learning, to test hypotheses or to examine issues. More able students can also be expected to use a variety of data-collection methods and to analyse their data using more advanced techniques including statistical tests. This is also likely to be an opportunity to make use of ICT. As has been emphasised in Chapter 4, students often thrive where they are allowed choice and autonomy, and a field visit may be an opportunity to encourage this, particularly if numbers are small. A programme organised and run by an individual geography department can offer a variety of activities which are particularly appropriate and challenging for more able pupils; enquiry skills are stimulated when a new and unfamiliar location is studied and often activities such as presentations enable pupils to bring together in the fieldwork location things that have been learnt over a period of time.

A note about risk assessment

Schools are required to have a member of staff who is designated as educational visits coordinator, who will work alongside teachers planning field trips to advise on school and local authority guidelines for facilitating outdoor learning safely. There are a number of DfEE and DfES publications which advise on good practice and responsibility for health and safety of pupils on educational visits. The Teachernet website provides information on school journeys and outdoor education centres and on health and safety on education visits. The Royal Geographical Society–Institute of British Geographers (RGS–IBG) website provides details of the Expedition Advisory Centre, which offers information, training and advice for anyone embarking on scientific or adventurous expeditions. (For a list of useful websites, see the Further Information chapter.)

Competitions and other projects

Many students welcome the chance to participate in competitions and activities, and this can be an opportunity for your more able students to be involved in something beyond the usual curriculum. Organisations such as the RGS, the Ordnance Survey (OS) and the Geographical Association (GA) all run geographical competitions and activities.

Each year, the RGS–IBG organise the Young Geographer of the Year competition. This was launched in 1999 'to promote the study of geography and to encourage students to carry out independent research alongside their usual studies.' Pupils from any school can enter in three categories: Junior Geographer (12 and under); Young Geographer (13–15 years); Senior Geographer (16–18 years). Entrants are usually asked to write about a topical issue.

The Geographical Association also encourages individuals and schools to get involved in competitions and activities through their 'Worldwise' initiative. Details are available on the GA website, together with notices about other geographical competitions. The OS also runs regular competitions via their website.

MetLinkInternational Weather Project is run by the Royal Meteorological Society. Participants around the world exchange weather observations using an online database, and they encourage anybody to be involved with the project, however simple their weather instruments. There is more information on their website.

Another idea is to encourage your most able to write an article about a local issue or a place they know well and to submit it for publication in *Wideworld* magazine, published by Philip Allan Updates and aimed at GCSE students.

Case study – Earth science essay writing competition

Holly entered a competition for prospective earth science students organised by Oxford University earth science department. She chose to write an essay called 'Earthquake prediction – a waste of time?' This enabled Holly to build on her existing knowledge and to explore the field of earthquake prediction in depth and to look at the relevance and reliability of earth science study in the modern world. It was an excellent opportunity for in-depth research and to develop some critical thinking skills. Holly came third in the competition and it was excellent preparation for later university interviews, including one at Oxford, as well as giving her a lot of personal satisfaction.

Enrichment and extension activities

Both extension and enrichment activities in geography can develop challenge to a high level. Extension, which adds breadth, can be a completely new intellectual domain that the pupil has not encountered before, a set of new learning skills that can be used to enhance the curriculum, or an aspect of the subject that is not part of the general taught syllabus. Enrichment is a deepening of the knowledge and understanding of a particular topic or theme. Geography departments will be looking to develop elements of both in everyday lessons to stretch their more able pupils, as discussed in Chapter 4, but it may be easier to develop rigour and challenge outside the confines of lessons. This may include activities run in school using lunchtimes or time after school.

Enrichment and extension activity – Fairtrade Fortnight, McAuley Catholic School, Doncaster

Teachers in the geography department worked with about 30 Year 7 students who had been identified by their geography teachers as the most able. The students worked on the project in their free time, deciding on how to promote Fairtrade around school during Fairtrade Fortnight. They decided on a range of activities including inviting a speaker from Fairtrade to speak in an assembly, designing posters and leaflets to put around school, doing a drama production and running a tuck shop selling Fairtrade produce. The students were encouraged to decide what should be done and to take responsibility for it and many of them worked very hard. They developed new skills, increased their confidence and raised over £1000 for Fairtrade through tuck shop sales. Awareness about issues surrounding fair trade was raised throughout the school.

Enrichment and extension activities can be run at weekends, after school and in holiday periods, where time can be spent going into more depth on particular topics, opportunities can be provided for more open-ended research and enquiry, and facilities such as ICT can be used when and where they are needed rather than when they are available! Outside speakers who can bring in a high level of expertise can contribute to these activities. Examples include challenge days, masterclasses and summer schools. Challenge days clearly have activities concentrated into one day, whereas masterclasses may be one-off events or may be a series of classes run over several weeks. Masterclasses would usually have input from an expert in the field. Summer schools generally extend over a number of days or even weeks during the summer holidays and may be focused on the pupils moving from primary to secondary school. Funding to run events such as these can come from a variety of sources. Support may be available through the local authority gifted and talented budget or from individual schools putting in their own funding. In some cases pupils may be charged a small amount to attend, but it is always important not to exclude those who cannot afford to pay. If schools work together, sending pupils to participate in a jointly organised event, then this can help to keep costs down. This 'hub' model, with one school hosting and other schools sending along their able geographers, is highly recommended because it gets more able pupils from different backgrounds, different age groups and different schools mixing and working together.

Challenge days and masterclasses

Levels of expertise, particular interests and qualifications among teachers in schools can often be an area of untapped potential. Similarly, there may be experts among the school governors or parents who would be willing to contribute to challenge days or masterclasses. Within school it is not always heads of geography who drive these activities. Colleagues on the staff who have joined teaching from other careers, advanced skills teachers (ASTs) and even newly qualified teachers (NQTs) may bring with them particular areas of geographical interest, expertise and enthusiasm which should be capitalised on.

Challenge day – Nobel School, Stevenage

In October 2003, a geography challenge day was held for North Hertfordshire at the Nobel School, Stevenage. Twelve local schools took part, each sending four Year 9 students. A representative for the Geographical Association's Valuing Places project helped the school to plan the day and led the sessions with the pupils. It was decided to plan a challenging geographical activity which would contain material new to most, if not all. The theme of 'Boundaries' was chosen, as it is important when studying place, and the main focus was on Kurdistan. The participants were put into groups and were given the task of analysing the Kurdish problems and promoting their own solutions to the situation as they saw it. Initial activities included a quiz, an exercise on what makes an effective boundary, and recognition of different types of boundaries with examples. The participants were given background information and briefing sheets and were asked to find solutions to this complex issue. The day was very successful and pupil feedback was very positive.

Challenge day – Marlborough School, St Albans

This challenge day organised for able Key Stage 3 geography students took the format of an enquiry surrounding a traffic management issue in the St Albans area. The day began with team-building and ice-breaking exercises, as the participating students were from several different schools. The main focus was on the issues surrounding a proposed new bypass around a local village, which is needed because of problems caused by large lorries travelling through the main village street. Students were involved in deciding for themselves the best route for the bypass to take.

A local resident, the MP for the area and a conservationist were asked to speak, putting forward the issues involved and drawing attention to the conflicts of interest. The enquiry route was then explained to the students who were encouraged to set aims and hypotheses, and to decide what data to collect and how to collect it. They were then taken to the village to carry out the fieldwork. On their return the groups spent time compiling a report and a cost/benefit analysis of the proposed bypass for their presentations.

It was a very enjoyable day and students found making their own decisions and choices about how to follow the enquiry a challenge. Hopefully this made them reflect on their learning and think critically about what they needed to do and why!!

Masterclass – Rickmansworth School, Hertfordshire

The geography department decided that it was important for pupils to have an understanding of how individual decisions have global effects and to be encouraged to investigate how their actions can have global consequences. The masterclasses were for Year 7 pupils and focused on the more able. First, some important processes and ideas about energy loss were explained, and then the pupils were asked to design houses that would be energy-efficient both inside and outside. Pupils enjoyed the sessions, extended their knowledge and understanding and became more independent learners.

Masterclass – Beaumont School, St Albans

This series of masterclasses was run over a six-month period, with five evening sessions and two full days during school holidays. The title was 'Ice, Fire and Climate' and included expert input from a geography lecturer from Hertfordshire University and a visit to the Scott Polar Research Institute at Cambridge University. Places studied included the Greenland ice sheet, Iceland and parts of the Russian Arctic, and pupils were introduced to simple statistical models and computer modelling techniques. Some comments afterwards included: 'I enjoyed working alongside new people with new ideas' and 'the speakers were great and it wasn't just a lecture, we were involved all the time.'

Summer schools

Because summer schools extend over a period of days or even weeks, there is a significant cost to consider as well as the large amount of work needed to organise them. For this reason, schools have often organised these with support from their local authority and sometimes by working with other schools. Until 2007, Standards Fund money was available and enabled schools to run their own summer schools with no cost to pupils. The money available covered all costs, including payment for the staff organising and delivering the activities. The main requirement for funding eligibility was that at least 50% of the participating pupils came from Year 6 in local primary schools, with an emphasis on transition. The last Standards Fund money available for these summer schools was in 2007, but schools and local authorities are expected to look for ways to enable summer schools to continue in the future through alternative sources of funding.

Summer schools are an ideal way to bring more able children together to work on projects and activities that enrich and extend their learning in ways that are not always possible or practical in normal lessons. Unlike one-off events, they give pupils the opportunity to develop their learning over an extended period of time and in a cohesive way. The results can be impressive. For incoming Year 7s, it is an excellent introduction to their secondary school career, and it can give more able pupils a flying start. For the staff involved, it is an opportunity to work in creative ways with motivated and very able pupils. Some summer schools are also built into the specialist status remit of individual secondary schools. Summer schools can focus on single subjects or themes but they can also enable links to be made to other curriculum areas.

Summer school – Stanborough School, Welwyn Garden City, Hertfordshire

'The Commonwealth of Welwyn Garden City' summer school ran over two weeks in 2002. In week 1, the pupils, working in groups as different Commonwealth countries, studied aspects such as the history and economy of those countries and visited their respective embassies in London. They carried out independent research and presented their findings to the rest of the pupils, and in subsequent days they explored aspects of Commonwealth culture such as silk batik painting, reggae music and poetry, and cooking different dishes! Week 2 was devoted to skills of research, discussion and debate, and public speaking, involving work in different committees and leading to a simulation of a Commonwealth Heads of Government Conference. This also provided a good opportunity to reinforce ideas about global citizenship and sustainability.

The programme for this summer school is given on the website.

Summer school – Chauncy School, Ware, Hertfordshire

The Chauncy School's well established 'Survival Geography' has proved successful in developing geographical knowledge and understanding in very practical and active ways. It is organised by the geography department and has helped to raise the profile of the subject within the school.

Until recently NAGTY ran summer schools and outreach courses suitable for geographers, for example those based at Field Studies Council centres. The CfBT are also promising to provide non-residential summer schools and a wide range of outreach provision, including summer activities, weekend events and online and blended learning models. These will be available to both members and non-members and there will be free places for the disadvantaged. More information can be found on the CfBT web site (www.cfbt.com).

Links with universities

Universities are increasingly being encouraged to work more closely with local schools and colleges. Some universities now organise masterclasses for the most able students in local sixth forms. These may be organised in association with the local authority, possibly through the Gifted and Talented or the Aimhigher wings of EiC. Schools may not be aware that universities have funding through the Aimhigher programme and that they are encouraged to organise events for local schools. It is worthwhile schools being proactive and making a direct approach to the geography department at their local university to see if they are willing to be involved in working with some of the most able pupils.

Some school geography departments already have close links with universities through Initial Teacher Training (ITT) partnerships or with the university geography department. This is another possible avenue for teachers to develop opportunities for their most able pupils, possibly through visits to the university or by arranging for ITT students to work with the more able within school.

Links with business and other organisations

Visiting experts

> One effective way of creating challenge is to introduce into the classroom an expert with skills which pupils may wish to emulate.

(Eyre 1997)

Making contact with businesses or other organisations can add both interest and first-hand information to the geography curriculum. The school may already have established links with local organisations, for example through work experience placements. It may not be possible to take pupils to visit places such as a local farm or factory, but an excellent alternative is to ask someone to come into school to talk to the pupils, as an 'expert'. This may be possible within lessons or perhaps as part of an extended assembly where a larger group of pupils can attend. Clearly it is better if this kind of input is integrated into the curriculum and is a regular feature rather than just a one-off event.

'Experts' might include a planner or environmental officer from the local council who could talk about a controversial local issue. Stimulating talks might also be given by someone who has worked abroad or travelled extensively, someone who is involved in development projects, perhaps with organisations such as Oxfam or Christian Aid, or someone involved with campaigns such as 'Fair Trade' or 'Drop the Debt'. 'Experts' do not always have to come from beyond the school community as many parents and indeed other members of staff may have expertise or experiences which they are willing to share. As an invited speaker these expert visitors often talk with great enthusiasm and capture the interest of pupils.

Visiting expert – Visit by a local farmer to the Minster School, Southwell

During their Year 8 unit 'Changing Agriculture', pupils learn about how farming has changed during the last fifty years and how this has affected people and the environment. As part of this unit, a local farmer is invited to speak to all classes about recent changes in dairy farming at his family-owned farm. The talk focuses on changes in technology, animal welfare, use of chemicals and the outputs of the farm; photographs and figures provide clear evidence of how and why the farm has changed. The presentation stimulates a lot of interest and usually provokes interesting questions from the pupils. The follow-up work is an extended piece of writing called 'Evaluating changes in farming since 1950', which is used as an assessment, and usually results in some high quality work, particularly from the most able. In future, the department intends to follow this activity up by organising visits to the farm for small numbers of more able and more interested pupils, so that they can see the farm in action and explore some of the issues in more depth. This is part of the local 'Leaf Project', which is working to improve public understanding of farming and encourages interaction with schools.

Opportunities for staff development

As well as providing opportunities for pupils, the local universities, businesses and other organisations can also provide opportunities for professional development for staff. The new YG&T Programme run by CfBT will include training for staff. The Geographical Association and the Royal Geographical Society (RGS/IBG) also offer professional development events including CPD courses and lectures.

Summary

- Outside-the-classroom activities including fieldwork, and links with universities, businesses and other organisations can stimulate interest and provide challenge for the most able.

- Fieldwork can help to stimulate a genuine interest in geography and provide opportunities for using sophisticated fieldwork techniques and incorporating some degree of choice and autonomy.

- Competitions can be a way for able pupils to develop a particular interest.

- Challenge days and masterclasses are excellent forms of enrichment and extension for the most able.

- Summer schools can provide challenge for the more able.

- Local universities may provide opportunities for more able pupils.

- Making use of visiting 'experts' to talk to pupils benefits all pupils, including the more able.

- It is important to look for opportunities for staff development as this is also an important element of making provision for the most able.

Appendices

Institutional quality standards in gifted and talented education

Generic Elements	Entry	Developing	Exemplary
	A – Effective teaching and learning strategies		
1. Identification	i. The school/college has learning conditions and systems to identify gifted and talented pupils in all year groups and an agreed definition and shared understanding of the meaning of 'gifted and talented' within its own, local and national contexts.	i. Individual pupils are screened annually against clear criteria at school/college and subject/topic level.	i. **Multiple criteria and sources of evidence** are used to identify gifts and talents, including through the use of a broad range of quantitative and qualitative data.
	ii. An **accurate record** of the identified gifted and talented population is kept and updated.	ii. The record is used to identify under-achievement and **exceptional achievement** (both within and outside the population) and to track/review pupil **progress**.	ii. The record is supported by a comprehensive monitoring, progress planning and reporting system which all staff regularly share and contribute to.
	iii. The identified gifted and talented population broadly reflects the school/college's **social and economic composition**, gender and ethnicity.	iii. **Identification** systems address issues of **multiple exceptionality** (pupils with specific gifts/talents and special educational needs).	iii. **Identification** processes are regularly reviewed and refreshed in the light of pupil performance and value-added data. The gifted and talented population is fully representative of the school/college's population.
Evidence			
Next steps			
2. Effective provision in the classroom	i. The school/college addresses the different needs of the gifted and talented population by providing a stimulating learning environment and by extending the teaching repertoire.	i. Teaching and learning strategies are diverse and flexible, meeting the needs of distinct pupil groups within the gifted and talented population (e.g. able underachievers, exceptionally able).	i. The school/college has established a range of methods to find out what works best in the classroom, and shares this within the school/college and with other schools and colleges.
	ii. Teaching and learning is differentiated and delivered through both individual and group activities.	ii. A range of challenging learning and teaching strategies is evident in lesson planning and delivery. **Independent learning** skills are developed.	ii. Teaching and learning are suitably challenging and varied, incorporating the breadth, depth and pace required to progress high achievement. Pupils routinely work independently and self-reliantly.

	Entry	Developing	Exemplary
	iii. Opportunities exist to extend learning through **new technologies**.	iii. The use of **new technologies** across the curriculum is focused on **personalised learning** needs.	iii. The innovative use of new technologies raises the achievement and motivation of gifted and talented pupils.
Evidence			
Next steps			
3. Standards	i. Levels of **attainment** and **achievement** for gifted and talented pupils are comparatively high in relation to the rest of the school/college population and are in line with those of similar pupils in similar schools/colleges.	i. Levels of **attainment** and **achievement** for gifted and talented pupils are broadly consistent across the gifted and talented population and above those of similar pupils in similar schools/colleges.	i. Levels of attainment and achievement for gifted and talented pupils indicate sustainability over time and are well above those of similar pupils in similar schools/colleges.
	ii. Self-evaluation indicates that gifted and talented provision is satisfactory.	ii. Self-evaluation indicates that gifted and talented provision is good.	ii. Self-evaluation indicates that gifted and talented provision is very good or excellent.
	iii. Schools/colleges' gifted and talented education programmes are explicitly linked to the achievement of SMART outcomes and these highlight improvements in pupils' attainment and achievement.		
Evidence			
Next steps			
B – Enabling curriculum entitlement and choice			
4. Enabling curriculum entitlement and choice	i. Curriculum organisation is flexible, with opportunities for enrichment and increasing subject/topic choice. Pupils are provided with support and guidance in making choices.	i. The curriculum offers opportunities and guidance to pupils which enable them to work beyond their age and/or phase, and across subjects or topics, according to their aptitudes and interests.	i. The curriculum offers personalised learning pathways for pupils which maximise individual potential, retain flexibility of future choices, extend well beyond test/examination requirements and result in sustained impact on pupil attainment and achievement.
Evidence			
Next steps			

Definitions for words and phrases in bold are provided in the glossary in the Quality Standards *User Guide*, available at www2.teachernet.gov.uk/gat. QS Model October 2005

Generic Elements	Entry	Developing	Exemplary
C – Assessment for learning			
5. Assessment for learning	i. Processes of data analysis and pupil assessment are employed throughout the school/college to plan learning for gifted and talented pupils.	i. Routine progress reviews, using both qualitative and quantitative data, make effective use of prior, predictive and value-added attainment data to plan for progression in pupils' learning.	i. Assessment data are used by teachers and across the school/college to ensure challenge and sustained progression in individual pupils' learning.
	ii. Dialogue with pupils provides focused feedback which is used to plan future learning.	ii. Systematic oral and written feedback helps pupils to set challenging curricular targets.	ii. Formative assessment and individual target setting combine to maximise and celebrate pupils' achievements.
	iii. Self and peer assessment, based on clear understanding of criteria, are used to increase pupils' responsibility for learning.	iii. Pupils reflect on their own skill development and are involved in the design of their own targets and tasks.	iii. Classroom practice regularly requires pupils to reflect on their own progress against targets, and engage in the direction of their own learning.
Evidence			
Next steps			
6. Transfer and transition	i. Shared processes, using agreed criteria, are in place to ensure the productive transfer of information from one setting to another (i.e. from class to class, year to year and school/college to school/college).	i. Transfer information concerning gifted and talented pupils, including parental input, informs targets for pupils to ensure progress in learning. Particular attention is given to including new admissions.	i. Transfer data concerning gifted and talented pupils are used to inform planning of teaching and learning at subject/aspect/topic and individual pupil level, and to ensure progression according to ability rather than age or phase.
Evidence			
Next steps			
D – School/college organisation			
7. Leadership	i. A named member of the governing body, senior management team and the lead professional responsible for gifted and talented education have clearly directed responsibilities for motivating and driving gifted and talented provision. The head teacher actively champions gifted and talented provision.	i. Responsibility for gifted and talented provision is distributed, and evaluation of its impact shared, at all levels in the school/college. Staff subscribe to policy at all levels. Governors play a significant supportive and evaluative role.	i. Organisational structures, communication channels and the deployment of staff (e.g. workforce remodelling) are flexible and creative in supporting the delivery of personalised learning. Governors take a lead in celebrating achievements of gifted and talented pupils.
Evidence			
Next steps			

8. Policy	i. The gifted and talented policy is integral to the school/college's inclusion agenda and approach to personalised learning, feeds into and from the single school/college improvement plan and is consistent with other policies.	i. The policy directs and reflects best practice in the school/college, is regularly reviewed and is clearly linked to other policy documentation.	i. The policy includes input from the whole school/college community and is regularly refreshed in the light of innovative national and international practice.
Evidence			
Next steps			
9. School/college ethos and pastoral care	i. The school/college sets high expectations, recognises achievement and celebrates the successes of all its pupils. ii. The school/college identifies and addresses the particular social and emotional needs of gifted and talented pupils in consultation with pupils, parents and carers.	i. The school/college fosters an environment which promotes positive behaviour for learning. Pupils are listened to and their views taken into account. ii. Strategies exist to counteract bullying and any adverse effects of social and curriculum pressures. Specific support for able underachievers and pupils from different cultures and social backgrounds is available and accessible.	i. An ethos of ambition and achievement is agreed and shared by the whole school/college community. Success across a wide range of abilities is celebrated. ii. The school/college places equal emphasis on high achievement and emotional well being, underpinned by programmes of support personalised to the needs of gifted and talented pupils. There are opportunities for pupils to use their gifts to benefit other pupils and the wider community.
Evidence			
Next steps			
10. Staff development	i. Staff have received professional development in meeting the needs of gifted and talented pupils.	i. The induction programme for new staff addresses gifted and talented issues, both at whole school/college and specific subject/aspect level.	i. There is ongoing audit of staff needs and an appropriate range of professional development in gifted and talented education. Professional development is informed by research and collaboration within and beyond the school/college.

Definitions for words and phrases in bold are provided in the glossary in the Quality Standards *User Guide*, available at www2.teachernet.gov.uk/gat. QS Model October 2005

© Crown Copyright 2005–2007.

Generic Elements	Entry	Developing	Exemplary
	ii. The lead professional responsible for gifted and talented education has received appropriate professional development.	ii. Subject/aspect and phase leaders have received specific professional development in meeting the needs of gifted and talented pupils.	ii. Priorities for the development of gifted and talented provision are included within a professional development entitlement for all staff and are monitored through performance management processes.
Evidence			
Next steps			
11. Resources	i. Provision for gifted and talented pupils is supported by appropriate budgets and resources.	i. Allocated resources include school/college based and nationally available resources, and these have a significant and measurable impact on the progress that pupils make and their attitudes to learning.	i. Resources are used to stimulate innovative and experimental practice, which is shared throughout the school/college and which are regularly reviewed for impact and best value.
Evidence			
Next steps			
12. Monitoring and evaluation	i. Subject and phase audits focus on the quality of teaching and learning for gifted and talented pupils. Whole school/college targets are set using prior attainment data.	i. Performance against targets (including at pupil level) is regularly reviewed. Targets include qualitative pastoral and curriculum outcomes as well as numerical data.	i. Performance against targets is rigorously evaluated against clear criteria. Qualitative and quantitative outcomes inform whole-school/college self-evaluation processes.
	ii. Elements of provision are planned against clear objectives within effective whole-school self-evaluation processes.	ii. All elements, including non-academic aspects of gifted and talented provision, are planned to clear objectives and are subjected to detailed evaluation.	ii. The school/college examines and challenges its own provision to inform development of further experimental and innovative practice in collaboration with other schools/colleges.
Evidence			
Next steps			

E – Strong partnerships beyond the school

	Entry	Developing	Exemplary
13. Engaging with the community, families and beyond	i. Parents/carers are aware of the school's/college's policy on gifted and talented provision, contribute to its identification processes and are kept informed of developments in gifted and talented provision, including through the School Profile. ii. The school/college shares good practice and has some collaborative provision with other schools, colleges and the wider community.	i. Progression of gifted and talented pupils is enhanced by home-school/college partnerships. There are strategies to engage and support hard-to-reach parents/carers. ii. A coherent strategy for networking with other schools, colleges and local community organisations extends and enriches provision.	i. Parents/carers are actively engaged in extending provision. Support for gifted and talented provision is integrated with other children's services (e.g. Sure Start, EAL, traveller, refugee, LAC Services). ii. There is strong emphasis on collaborative and innovative working with other schools/colleges which impacts on quality of provision locally, regionally and nationally.
Evidence			
Next steps			
14. Learning beyond the classroom	i. There are opportunities for pupils to learn beyond the school/college day and site (extended hours and out-of-school activities). ii. Pupils participate in dedicated gifted and talented activities (e.g. summer schools) and their participation is recorded.	i. A coherent programme of enrichment and extension activities (through extended hours and out-of-school activities) complements teaching and learning and helps identify pupils' latent gifts and talents. ii. Local and national provision helps meet individual pupils' learning needs, e.g. NAGTY membership, accessing outreach, local enrichment programmes.	i. Innovative models of learning beyond the classroom are developed in collaboration with local and national schools/colleges to further enhance teaching and learning. ii. Coherent strategies are used to direct and develop individual expert performance via external agencies, e.g. HE/FE links, online support, and local/regional/national programmes.
Evidence			
Next steps			

Definitions for words and phrases in bold are provided in the glossary in the Quality Standards *User Guide*, available at www2.teachernet.gov.uk/gat. QS Model October 2005

© Crown Copyright 2005–2007.

Geography provision – a checklist for consideration

	Focus question	Yes/No/In progress	Priority for action
1	Has the department developed a policy on its provision for the more able students?		
2	Does it have a more able/G&T coordinator or representative who liaises directly with the school coordinator?		
3	Are the more able students clearly identified in subject registers?		
4	Has the department identified CPD requirements in relation to more able students?		
5	Has the department agreed the strategies it will use to provide suitable pace, depth and breadth for the most able?		
6	Does the department have an agreed approach to providing for the exceptional child whose needs might not easily be met in the general classroom?		
7	Does short/medium-term planning outline expectations for the most able and any extended/ modified tasks for them?		
8	Are there suitable resources for the most able?		
9	Is homework used to extend the most able?		
10	Do the most able have plenty of opportunities to develop as independent learners?		
11	Are different learning styles taken into account when planning for and assessing the most able? Are appropriate AfL strategies used?		
12	Do you keep a portfolio of evidence for work in the department?		
13	Is provision for the most able regularly discussed at development meetings? Are schemes of work reviewed to ensure provision?		
14	Do you share good practice in more able provision with other departments or schools?		
15	Is the progress of your most able students effectively monitored?		

(based on audit documentation from Bramcote Hills School)

From *Meeting the Needs of Your Most Able Pupils: Geography*, Routledge 2007

An audit of provision for more able students in geography

Year	Challenge Thinking skills Independent and collaborative	High quality talk Presentations Questioning Leadership	Transforming information Work self-ownership Creative thinking Original writing	Purpose Relevance/audience Contributions to society (local to global)	Metacognition Learning to learn Skill development Transferability
7					
8					
9					

(based on David Leat's model for effective provision (Leat 1998))

From *Meeting the Needs of Your Most Able Pupils: Geography*, Routledge 2007

Audit of learning styles with focus on provision for more able students

Learning tool	Year 7	Year 8	Year 9
Thinking skills			
Problem solving			
Analysis			
Critical thinking			
Presentation			
Group leadership			
Extended writing			
Report writing			
Independent learning			
Peer assessment			

From *Meeting the Needs of Your Most Able Pupils: Geography*, Routledge 2007

Geography department action plan for improving provision for more able students (annual)

Priority	Actions	When	By whom?	Success criteria	Resource implications
1					Review date
2					Review date
3					Review date

Appendix 2.4

Lesson observation schedule: gifted & talented focus

School: _____   Age of students: _____
Date/Time: _____   Lesson observed: _____
Teacher: _____   Observer: _____

Planned teaching	Planned learning
Appropriate curriculum	Thinking skills
Differentiation for individuals	Questioning skills
Pace/Challenge/Style	Initiative/Responsibility for learning
Grouping/Seating arrangements	Task commitment
Opportunities for discussion	Assessment for learning
Opportunities for creativity	Enrichment/Enhancement/Acceleration

(based on Norfolk G&T Task Group, May 2003)

 From *Meeting the Needs of Your Most Able Pupils: Geography*, Routledge 2007

Monitoring and evaluation: student work analysis feedback

Student work analysis feedback		
Geography department	Subject leader:	Date:
Focus students	Comments on most able	
Is there an appropriate range of tasks evident in the student work?		
Do the tasks sufficiently challenge the more able students?		
Is there evidence of appropriate expectations of student work?		
Do more able students achieve more or less well in relation to expectations?		
Do students demonstrate a progressive increase in standards?		
Is there evidence of students demonstrating initiative in their work?		

From *Meeting the Needs of Your Most Able Pupils: Geography*, Routledge 2007

Monitoring and evaluation: scheme of work feedback

Scheme of work feedback		
Geography department	**Subject leader:**	**Date:**
Focus	**Comments**	
Does the scheme of work provide sufficient opportunities for more able students?		
Does the scheme of work identify what all pupils need to know, understand and be able to do to reach the highest levels?		
Does guidance on differentiation address the needs of the more able students?		
Are there arrangements for moving onto more advanced work?		
Are sufficient resources available to facilitate the delivery of the scheme of work for the more able students in all classes?		
Does assessment challenge the more able students? Is appropriate guidance and feedback given?		

 From *Meeting the Needs of Your Most Able Pupils: Geography*, Routledge 2007

Geography progress record

<table>
<tr><td colspan="2" align="center">Year 9 Key Stage 3</td></tr>
<tr><td>Name: _____</td><td>Form: _____</td></tr>
<tr><td colspan="2">My Year 9 Geography Target is [ ]</td></tr>
</table>

Year 9 Autumn Term   **Natural Environment/Rainforest**   **AP1**

Effort	Attainment	Achievements, Strengths and Areas to Improve
A B C D E	NC Level 8 7 6 5 4 3	 Initial

Year 9 Spring Term   **Development & Globalisation**   **AP2**

Effort	Attainment	Achievements, Strengths and Areas to Improve
A B C D E	NC Level 8 7 6 5 4 3	 Initial

Year 9 Summer Term   **Contrasting Nations & Migration**   **AP3**

Effort	Attainment	Achievements, Strengths and Areas to Improve
A B C D E	NC Level 8 7 6 5 4 3	 Initial

Effort Scale:
A – Excellent   You have consistently worked very hard, tried your best with maximum effort.
B – Very Good   You have worked well and usually shown very good effort.
C – Satisfactory   You have made a reasonable effort which is adequate.
D – Unsatisfactory   You have made a poor effort and more is needed. You are underperforming.
E – Very Poor   You have made minimal, if any, effort. This is a serious concern.

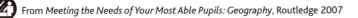

From *Meeting the Needs of Your Most Able Pupils: Geography*, Routledge 2007

Monitoring and evaluation: departmental review and report

Evaluation report: More able provision		
Geography department	Subject leader	Date
Summary of strengths and areas for development		
Focus	Comments on most able students	
Whole-school or cross-curricular links		

Geography department: individual pupil checklist

Name _____ Class _____ Teacher _____

Characteristic	Evidence/notes
A fascination with places; wide-ranging general knowledge about the world and enjoyment of learning more	
Well developed sense of place; ability to draw on theories and models to explain patterns and processes and understand the interdependence of places	
Can apply geographical knowledge and understanding to new and unfamiliar contexts	
The ability to select and make effective use of a wide range of geographical skills and techniques to support investigations and clearly communicate the findings	
Can rapidly assimilate and synthesise new information to aid analysis	
Ability to explain complex interactions and relationships within and between human and physical processes	
Making use of a wide and precise geographical vocabulary and terminology	
Ability to predict and explain changes in the characteristics of places over time	
Asking perceptive, linked and complex geographical questions	
Expressing a range of viewpoints about an issue; highly developed and sensitive values system	
Creative and original thinking	
Proficient in undertaking independent working and enquiry	
Works well collaboratively and in less formal teaching situations (e.g. field trips)	
Can critically evaluate geographical evidence and enquiry and suggest improvements	
Understands links with other subjects and can transfer knowledge and skills	

From *Meeting the Needs of Your Most Able Pupils: Geography*, Routledge 2007

Rapid checklist for identifying more able pupils in geography

Rapidly – without thinking too much – write in the names of the pupils in your class who spring to mind as you consider the descriptions below. It is not essential that every description has a name attached to it.

Description	Pupils' names
Asks challenging questions	
Provocative	
Uses language confidently and creatively; has a feeling for words	
Wide general/geographic knowledge; contributes wealth of ideas and information	
Speculates, suggests and predicts	
Has spatial awareness	
Intense curiosity	
Logical, systematic approach to tasks	
Sees relationships	
Inventive, enjoys experimentation	
Stream of 'why' and 'how' questions	
Wide vocabulary	
Absorbed in books	
Shows empathy with others	
Highly sensitive	
Fiercely self-critical	
Fascination with numbers and figures	
Bored by repetition	
Instinctive learner – dislikes rote memory tasks	
Creative, original thinker	
Self-directed	

 From *Meeting the Needs of Your Most Able Pupils: Geography*, Routledge 2007

VAK Questionnaire for use with pupils

Which sense do you prefer to learn with?

Situation: When you . . .	Your preferred course of action: Do you . . .		
	Visual	**Auditory**	**Kinaesthetic**
Spell a word	Try to visualise it (Does it look right?)	Sound it out (Does it sound right?)	Write it down (Does it feel right?)
Are concentrating	Get most distracted by untidiness	Get most distracted by noise	Get most distracted by noise or physical disturbance
Choose a favourite art form	Prefer paintings	Prefer music	Prefer dance/ sculpture
Reward someone	Tend to write praise on their work in a note	Tend to give them oral praise	Tend to give them a pat on the back
Talk	Talk quite fast, but keep idle conversation limited. Use lots of images e.g 'It's like looking for a needle in a haystack.'	Talk fluently with an even pace, in a logical order, with few hesitations and clear enunciation	Use lots of hand movements, talk about actions and feelings, speak more slowly with longer pauses
Meet people	Remember mostly how they looked/the surroundings	Remember mostly what was said/ their names	Remember mostly what you did with them/their emotions
See a movie, tv or read a novel	Remember best what the scenes/people looked like	Remember best what was said/how the music sounded	Remember best what happened/the characters' emotions
Relax	Generally prefer reading/tv	Generally prefer music	Generally prefer games, sport
Try to interpret someone's mood	Mainly note their facial expressions	Listen to their tone of voice	Watch body movements
Are recalling something	Remember what you saw/people's faces/how things looked	Remember what was said/ people's names/jokes	Remember what was done/what it felt like
Are memorising something	Prefer to memorise by writing something repeatedly	Prefer to memorise by repeating words aloud	Prefer to memorise by doing something repeatedly
Are choosing clothes	Choose almost exclusively by how they look, how they coordinate and by the colours	Take a lot of notice of the brand name, what the clothes 'say' about you	Choose mainly on how they feel, the comfort, the texture
Are angry	Become silent and seethe	Express it in an outburst	Storm about, clench your fists, throw things
Are inactive	Look around, doodle, watch something	Talk to yourself or others	Fidget, walk about

Situation: When you . . .	Your preferred course of action: Do you . . .		
Express yourself	Often use phrases like: I see/I get the picture/Let's shed some light on this/ I can picture it	Often use phrases like: That sounds right/I hear you/ That rings a bell/ Something tells me/It suddenly clicked/That's music to my ears	Often use phrases like: That feels right/ I'm groping for an answer/I've got a grip on it/I need a concrete example
Contact people on business	Prefer face-to-face contact	Rely on the telephone	Talk it out while walking, eating, etc.
Are learning	Prefer to read, to see the words, illustrations diagrams, sketch it out	Like to be told, attend lectures, talk it over	Like to get involved, hands on, try it out, write notes
Assemble new equipment	First look at the diagrams/read the instructions	First ask someone to tell you what to do	First work with the pieces
	And then your second choice would be to . . .		
	Ask questions/talk to yourself (A) as you assemble it and then do it (K)	Ask them to show you (V) and then try it (K)	Ask questions (A) and then look at the diagrams/ instructions (V)
Total responses			

Taken from *Teaching and Learning in Secondary Schools: Pilot. Unit 10: Learning Styles* (DfES 0350/2003)

An open-ended task incorporating choice and encouraging research

Pole to Pole

Imagine you are making a journey from the North Pole to the South Pole. You should chose a line of longitude to travel along. It must be a line that passes through at least five countries. Use the lessons in the library to find out about the countries you will be travelling through. You could also find out information from CDs, the internet and travel brochures or you could even use your own holiday experiences.

You must write about the places you saw, the people you met and the adventures you had. You could write a diary or send e-mails from internet cafes on your route. You could send home a postcard from each country or tape your adventures. You must include a map of your route and, if possible, maps of the countries you visit.

Have a good trip!

This exercise was devised by the geography department, King Edward VII School, Sheffield (it is also referred to in Roberts 2003). It was devised for use with Year 7s but could be adapted for older pupils.

Scheme of Work – Key Stage 3: Development and Globalisation Year 9 – Time: 8 Lessons

Learning Objectives	Learning Outcomes	Methodology/T&L Styles (VAK)	Available Resources
Knowledge and Understanding ● To recognise the terms MEDC/LEDC ● To use the measures of development to distinguish between MEDCs and LEDCs ● To investigate the relationships between various economic indicators ● To appreciate the interdependence of nations ● To be introduced to the concept of globalisation of industry	**All:** Will recognise basic terminology for poorer LEDC and richer MEDC nations. They will be able to remember at least three ways to distinguish between them. They will be able to describe the relationship between development indicators and be able to offer some simple explanations. They will begin to appreciate how nations are interdependent and that we live in a global society. They will be able to carry out basic research into globalised companies and report about them.	Discussion and questioning Whole class Individual guided tasks **Visual** Graphs, charts, maps and diagrams, photographs **Auditory** Spoken discussion, question and answer, listening skills **Kinaesthetic** Graph construction, webquest and collaborative PowerPoint presentation	● Duplicated worksheets in room 54 ● Text: Geog Matters 3 pages 5–14 and 44 onwards ● Text: Waugh connections pp 86–87 ● ICT facilities ● Globalisation webquest on school network ● Video: World 2000 Tp 83
Skills ● Recognition of key words ● Using economic measurements ● Graphing relationships between indicators + analysis ● Web-based research using webquest approach ● Collaborative PowerPoint presentation design ● Report writing	**Most:** Will have achieved all the ideas above and expanded into more detail. They will know a greater range of development indicators and both describe and explain relationships that exist between them. They will understand the issues of globalisation in more detail and be able to use specific examples and report on them, making good use of web-based material and different presentation styles.	**Cross Curricular** **Literacy** Specific terminology Explanatory and report writing Collaborative communication skills **Numeracy** Scatter graph construction and analysis **Thinking skills** Information processing Reasoning Creative thinking **Citizenship** Global citizenship **ICT** Globalisation of industry webquest PowerPoint presentation design GIS for measures of development and economic indicators	**Homework** ● Mind map of economic indicators ● Scatter graph analysis and discussion ● Examples of globalisation in society (e.g. the fashion industry) ● Collaborative presentation work **Assessments** ● Level of development quick test ● Globalisation report/article. Level and effort grade using standardised grid
Health and Safety Classroom based	**Some:** Will achieve all the above and develop a more comprehensive knowledge about the characteristics of MEDCs and LEDCs. They will be able to describe and explain fully the interdependence between nations and give examples. They will also appreciate the globalisation of society more fully, again using examples to get across their understanding, providing a fuller picture of comparison and contrast. Based on web-based research. They will take the lead in the reporting and presentation of globalised issues.	**SEN** Support materials and differentiated sheets (Folens)	

From the Minster School, Southwell, Nottinghamshire

From *Meeting the Needs of Your Most Able Pupils: Geography*, Routledge 2007

Extended writing task based on card-sorting exercise

Should the cliffs at Overstrand be protected?

Describe and explain what is happening to the cliffs at Overstrand on the Norfolk coast, and think about whether they could or should be protected to stop collapse in the future. You should:

- use as many geographical terms as you can

- include maps and diagrams in your answer to explain your ideas

- give your own opinion about cliff protection with reasons to justify yourself.

Many farms and even whole villages have disappeared into the sea since Roman times.	The land in this area is good agricultural land, but many farmers make extra money by providing services for tourists.
In 1973, there was over 150 metres between some houses at Overstrand and the sea; now there is only 25 metres in places.	The cliffs on the Norfolk coast are made of very weak and easily eroded rocks called boulder clay or till.
The prevailing winds are from the north-east, causing strong longshore drift from north to south.	Sea walls are very expensive to build and to maintain, but they are the best way of protecting the cliffs.
The material eroded from the cliffs by the sea is carried to other places such as the Thames Estuary and even to Holland.	It is difficult for some families in Overstrand to sell their houses and in some cases the value of their houses has fallen by over 50%.
Actions in one place have knock on effects elsewhere.	There are groynes along the beach at Overstrand.
The coast road at Overstrand had to be re-built because a section fell into the sea in 1992.	Rainwater soaks into the boulder clay cliffs which rapidly become unstable and collapse.
The Norfolk coast is one of the fastest eroding coasts in the world. On average, 2 to 3 metres per year disappears into the sea.	Some people think these cliffs can never be protected and they should be left to fall into the sea. The people who live there would have to move.
One of the main problems is underground water in the cliffs. The council are finding out about ways to drain the cliffs and make them more stable.	The sea makes the problem worse by removing landslide material. If there was a bigger beach it would form natural protection for the cliffs.
In May 1990, 45 metres of the cliff at Overstrand collapsed into the sea.	In some areas the council have prohibited new buildings near the cliff top.

N.B. This exercise should be supported with photographs or a video and an OS map extract.

From *Meeting the Needs of Your Most Able Pupils: Geography*, Routledge 2007

Webquest: Nike (clothing) – are they just doing it?

Task 1

- Describe briefly the history of Nike. When and where did the company begin?

- Where are the headquarters of Nike?

- What products does Nike produce?

- How is Nike recognised (logo/slogan)?

- Describe the image of the product and company.

- Which sportsman/woman is used to promote the company's products? How much could he/she be paid?

- In which countries is the product sold? Are these countries MEDCs or LEDCs?

www.nike.com/main.html (home page)
www.cafod.org.uk
news.bbc.co.uk (search Nike)
www.sportzwear.com (product prices)
www.globalexchange.org/economy/corporations/nike
www.google.co.uk (search for Nike in Google image search)

Task 2

- In which countries is the product produced? Are these MEDCs or LEDCs?

- How do the working conditions (pay, hours of work and working environment) compare with manufacturing conditions in MEDCs?

- What other issues surround the manufacture of the product in LEDCs?

- Is the product sold in the countries where it is made? If not, why not?

- If there are any negative issues surrounding Nike, what has the company done to change its image?

www.globalexchange.org/economy/corporations/nike/faq.html (shows where Nike manufactures trainers)
cbae.nmsu.edu/~dboje/nike/images/Image4.gif (manufacturing by country)
www.globalissues.org (search Nike)
www.nike.com
www.cleanclothes.org (search links to Nike)

www.oxfam.or.av (search sweatshops)
www.bbc.co.uk (search Nike sweatshops)

Task 3

From what you now understand about the products and Nike, discuss the issues that concern:

- the people (labour) in the LEDCs who manufacture the products

- the consumer in MEDCs.

www.globalexchange.org/economy/corporations/ (Nike and Gap)
www.globaleye.org.uk/secondary_summer/focuson/index.html (globalisation)
www.savethechildren.org.uk (search Nike)
www.thepetitionsite.com/takeaction (search Nike)

From a unit devised by the Minster School, Southwell, Nottinghamshire

References

Black, P., Harrison, C., Lee, C., Marshall, B. and Wiliam, D. (2003) *Assessment for Learning. Putting it into Practice.* Maidenhead: Open University Press.

Bloom, B. (ed.) (1956) *Taxonomy of Educational Objectives.* New York: Longmans, Green & Co.

Butt, G. (2000) *Reflective Teaching of Geography 11–18.* London: Continuum.

Butt, G. (2001) *Extending Writing Skills.* Sheffield: Geographical Association.

Davies, P. (1995) 'An inductive approach to levels of attainment', *International Response in Geographical and Environmental Education* (IRGEE), 4, 47–65.

Department for Education and Employment (1997) *Excellence in Schools.* London: DfEE.

Department for Education and Employment (1998) *Health and Safety of Pupils on Educational Visits: A Good Practice Guide.* London: DfEE.

Department for Education and Employment (1999) *Geography: The National Curriculum for England.* London: DfEE.

Department for Education and Skills (2001) *Health and Safety: Responsibilities and Powers.* 0803/2001. London: DfES.

Department for Education and Skills (2002) *Standards for Adventure. Supplement to Health and Safety of Pupils on Educational Visits: A Good Practice Guide.* 0565/2002. London: DfES.

Department for Education and Skills (2002) *Standards for LEAs in Overseeing Educational Visits. Supplement to Health and Safety of Pupils on Educational Visits: A Good Practice Guide.* 0564/2002. London: DfES.

Department for Education and Skills (2003) *Teaching and Learning in Secondary Schools: Pilot Unit 10. Learning Styles.* 0350/2003. London: DfES.

Department for Education and Skills (2004) *Schools Facing Challenging Circumstances.* London: DfES.

Eyre, D. (1997) *Able Children in Ordinary Schools.* London: David Fulton Publishers.

Eyre, D. and Lowe, H. (eds) (2002) *Curriculum Provision for the Gifted and Talented in the Secondary School.* London: David Fulton Publishers.

Fisher, D. and Binns, T. (eds) (2000) *Issues in Geography Teaching.* London: RoutledgeFalmer.

Fisher, R. (1998) *Teaching Thinking – Philosophical Enquiry in the Classroom.* London: Cassell.

Gardner, H. (1993) *Frames of Mind: The Theory of Multiple Intelligences* (10th annual edn.), New York: Basic Books.

Gardner, H. (1999) *Intelligence Reframed: Multiple Intelligences for the 21st Century.* New York: Basic Books.

George, D. (2003) *Gifted Education Identification and Provision* (2nd edn). London: David Fulton Publishers.

Ginnis, P. (2002) *The Teacher's Toolkit.* Carmarthen: Crown House Publishing.

Hicks, D. (1994) *Educating for the Future: A Practical Classroom Guide*. Godalming: WWF-UK.

Hughes, M. (1997) *Lessons are for Learning*. Stafford: Network Educational Press.

Job, D. (1996) 'Geography and environmental education – an exploration of perspectives and strategies' in Kent, A., Lambert, D., Naish, M. and Slater, F. (eds), *Geography in Education: Viewpoints on Teaching and Learning*. Cambridge: CUP.

Lambert, D. and Balderstone, D. (2000) *Learning to Teach Geography in the Secondary School*. London: RoutledgeFalmer.

Leat, D. (ed.) (1998) *Thinking Through Geography*. Cambridge: Chris Kington Publishing.

Lunzer, E. and Gardner, K. (1979) *The Effective Use of Reading*. Oxford: Heinemann.

Montgomery, D. (2003) *Gifted and Talented Children with Special Educational Needs. Double Exceptionality*. London: David Fulton Publishers.

Nichols, A. and Kinninment, D. (eds) (2001) *More Thinking Through Geography*. Cambridge: Chris Kington Publishing.

Ofsted (2003) *Handbook for Inspecting Secondary Schools*. London: Ofsted.

Ofsted (2003) *Inspection of Local Education Authorities. Ofsted/Audit Commission Inspection Guidance*. December 2003 v1a. London: Ofsted.

Ofsted (2004) *Subject Reports 2002/03. Geography in Secondary Schools*. London: Ofsted.

Renzulli, J. S. (1977) *The Enrichment Triad Model: A Guide for Developing Defensible Programs for the Gifted and Talented*. Mansfield Center, CT: Creative Learning Press.

Roberts, M. (2003) *Learning Through Enquiry: Making Sense of Geography in the Key Stage 3 Classroom*. Sheffield: Geographical Association.

Smith, A. (1996) *Accelerated Learning in the Classroom*. Stafford: Network Educational Press.

Swift, D. (ed.) (2005) *Meeting Special Educational Needs in the Curriculum: Geography*. London: David Fulton Publishers.

Swartz, R. J. and Parks, S. (1994) *Infusing the Teaching of Critical and Creative Instruction: A Lesson Design*. Pacific Grove, CA: Critical Thinking Press.

Teacher Training Agency (1998) *The National Standards for Subject Leaders*. London: TTA.

Wallace, B. (2000) *Teaching the Very Able Child*. London: David Fulton Publishers.

Weeden, P., Winter, J. and Broadfoot, P. (2002) *Assessment: What's in it for Schools?* London: RoutledgeFalmer.

Further information

Useful websites

Aimhigher www.aimhigher.ac.uk

DfES Gifted and Talented www.standards.dfes.gov.uk/giftedandtalented

DfES Key Stage Three Strategy www.standards.dfes.gov.uk

Field Studies Council www.field-studies-council.org

Geographical Association www.geography.org

Innovating with Geography www.qca.org.uk/ geography

London Gifted and Talented www.londongt.org.uk

MetLinkInternational Weather Project www.metlink.org/

National Academy for Gifted and Talented Youth www.nagty.ac.uk

National Association for Able Children in Education www.nace.co.uk

National Association for Gifted Children www.nagcbritain.org.uk

Neighbourhood Statistics (NeSS) www.neighbourhood.statistics.gov.uk

Ofsted www.ofsted.gov.uk

Ordnance Survey www.mapzone.co.uk/index.htm

QCA guidance on teaching Gifted and Talented www.nc.uk.net/gt/

RGS–IBG www.rgs.org

Specialist Schools Trust www.specialistschools.org.uk

Teachernet www.teachernet.gov.uk/visits

World Class Tests www.worldclassarena.org.uk